PHYSICALISM,
OR SOMETHING NEAR ENOUGH

¶MP

PRINCETON MONOGRAPHS

IN PHILOSOPHY

Harry Frankfurt, Series Editor

——————————— ⁋MℙP ———————————

The Princeton Monographs in Philosophy series
offers short historical and systematic studies
on a wide variety of philosophical topics.

PHYSICALISM, OR SOMETHING NEAR ENOUGH

Jaegwon Kim

PRINCETON UNIVERSITY PRESS

PRINCETON AND OXFORD

Copyright © 2005 by Princeton University Press
Published by Princeton University Press,
41 William Street, Princeton, New Jersey 08540
In the United Kingdom: Princeton University Press,
3 Market Place, Woodstock, Oxfordshire OX20 1SY
All Rights Reserved

Third printing, and first paperback printing, 2008
Paperback ISBN: 978-0-691-13385-0

The Library of Congress has cataloged the cloth edition of this
book as follows

Kim, Jaegwon.
Physicalism, or something near enough / Jaegwon Kim.
p. cm.—(Princeton monographs in philosophy)
Includes bibliographical references and index.
ISBN 0-691-11375-0 (hardcover: alk. paper)
1. Philosophy of mind. 2. Mind and body. I. Title. II. Series.

BD418.3.K55 2005
128'.2—dc22
2004053451

British Library Cataloging-in-Publication Data is available

This book has been composed in Janson
Printed on acid-free paper. ∞
press.princeton.edu

Printed in the United States of America

5 7 9 10 8 6 4

For

Nam Kyun, Yeong Min (IN MEMORIAM),
Yung Chul,
and Jae Won—the gang of four

Contents

Preface

I OFFER HERE no startlingly new views about the mind-body problem beyond what can be found in my earlier book *Mind in a Physical World* (MIT Press, 1998). Apart from some new material, on topics like substance dualism, the idea of reductive explanation, and the explanatory arguments for type physicalism, what the book does offer, I hope, is better focused and motivated arguments and a more clearly articulated overall view of the philosophical terrain involved. By and large I feel comfortable with the outcome, as it is presented here, of my toils and travails over the years; it is the kind of picture I feel I can live with, although there still are murky nooks and crannies that might harbor hidden difficulties and dangers.

As detailed below, all the chapters save chapter 2 originated as stand-alone lectures, and this meant that each had to be made largely intelligible on its own, with minimal references to outside sources. I have decided to preserve this character for each chapter. The six chapters of this book, therefore, are intended to be readable as independent essays as well as serve as links in the overall argument of the book. This, I believe, has both advantages and disadvantages. One advantage is that the reader can go over the book pretty much in any order he or she pleases, or pick the chapters that look interesting or promising. But there is also the disadvantage that, although I have tried to minimize this, there inevitably remains some overlap of material from chapter to chapter (for example, similar material on reduction will be found in chapters 1, 4, and 6). I hope, though, that this does not obscure the overall structure of the book's arguments. (In this regard the reader might find the "Synopsis of the Arguments" helpful.)

The material presented in chapters 1, 3, 4, and 6 derives in part from a series of five lectures given as the Daewoo Lectures, in Seoul, Korea, in the fall of 2000, under the auspices of the Korea Academic Research Council with the support of the Chosun Ilbo. I am grateful to the director of KARC, Dr. Yong Joon Kim, for the invitation and to its staff for cordial and efficient support. I also want to thank the many dozen philosophers in Seoul who participated in the events as commentators, discussants, translators, and chairs.

Chapters 2 and 5 are based on the Taft Lectures delivered at the University of Cincinnati in the spring of 2003. I am grateful to Tom Polger, John Bickle, Bob Richardson, Don Gustafson, and other members of the U.C. philosophy department for their hospitality and stimulating discussion.

An early version of chapter 1 appeared as "Mental Causation and Consciousness: the Two Mind-Body Problems for the Physicalist" in *Physicalism and Its Discontents*, edited by Carl Gillett and Barry Loewer (Cambridge University Press, 2001; used here with permission). Chapter 2 was originally prepared as a reply to Ned Block's "Do Causal Powers Drain Away?" and appeared under the title "Blocking Causal Drainage and Other Maintenance Chores with Mental Causation" in *Philosophy and Phenomenological Research* in July, 2003 (used with permission). An earlier version of chapter 3, with the title "Lonely Souls: Causality and Substance Dualism", was included in *Soul, Body, and Survival*, edited by Kevin Corcoran (Cornell University Press, 2001). A version of chapter 6 was given at the 2002 Wittgenstein Symposium in Kirchberg, Austria, and appears in the conference proceedings for that year. A similar version will appear as part of my contribution, "The Mind-Body Problem at Century's Turn," to *The Future of Philosophy*, edited by Brian Leiter, forthcoming from Oxford University Press.

I am indebted to Chris Hill, Terry Horgan, and Brian McLaughlin for valuable comments on chapter 5. My research assistant, Maura Geisser, has given me her usual dependable and efficient help. I am particularly grateful to Ian Malcolm, my editor at Princeton University Press, who has provided me with unfailingly friendly encouragement and capable support.

Synopsis of the Arguments

A STRONG PHYSICALIST outlook has shaped contemporary discussions of the mind-body problem. The aim of this book is to assess, after half a century of debate, just what kind of physicalism, or "how much" physicalism, we can lay claim to. My conclusion is that although we cannot have physicalism *tout court*, we can have something nearly as good.

Chapter 1 introduces the two principal challenges confronting contemporary physicalism. They are mental causation and consciousness. The problem of mental causation is to explain how mentality can have a causal role in a world that is fundamentally physical. The supervenience/exclusion argument shows that within a physicalist scheme, mental causation is possible only if mental phenomena are physically reducible. But is the mental reducible to the physical? In particular, can we give a reductive physicalist account of consciousness? This is the problem of consciousness. There are well-known, though by no means uncontested, reasons for thinking that phenomenal, or qualitative, consciousness cannot be physically reduced. In this way the two issues, mental causation and consciousness, become interlocked: the problem of mental causation is solvable only if mentality is physically reducible; however, phenomenal consciousness resists physical reduction, putting its causal efficacy in peril.

Chapter 2 presents a more detailed and improved formulation of the supervenience/exclusion argument, including an explanation of its fundamental motivating idea. The argument is divided into two stages, each with a philosophical moral of its own, and I show that there are two materially different ways of completing the second stage. Two of the more important objections raised against the argument are discussed. The first concerns the overdetermination option. The proposal is that we accept any purported physical effect of a mental event as overdetermined by two sufficient causes, one mental and one physical. I reject this suggestion. The second objection claims that the supervenience argument proves too much— specifically that, if correct, it would show that either all causation drains down to the bottom level of microphysics, depriving all special sciences of causality, or, if there is no bottom microlevel, there can be no causation anywhere. This is the "causal drainage" argument. I offer a two-pronged reply. First, the supervenience argument, I remind the reader, has been designed as a reductio against antireductionism; its point is that antireductionism, in conjunction with certain plausible principles and propositions, entails mental epiphenomenalism, a conclusion most of us are strongly inclined to reject. If the drainage objection works, it only adds to the force of the reductio. Second, the drainage argument is shown to depend on some questionable assumptions. Thus, chapters 1 and 2 lay out mental causation and consciousness as the two central problems for the contemporary physicalist, and then motivate and strengthen the supervenience argument. This prepares the starting point of the overall dialectic of the book.

Ontological dualism positing immaterial minds has not been taken seriously in contemporary philosophy of mind. Possibly as a response to the difficulties posed by mental causation and consciousness, however, the dualist approach is now showing signs of a revival. In chapter 3, I take a backward look at the idea of minds as immaterial substances, to argue that the dualism of material bodies and immaterial minds is not a workable option for anyone. For this purpose I formulate a causal argument.

This argument shows that immaterial minds, if they existed, would be incapable of entering into any causal relations, whether with material things or with other immaterial minds. This makes them gratuitous posits with no explanatory purpose to serve. The discussion provides concrete content to the oft-expressed complaint that, on account of their "diverse" natures, it is difficult to conceive how immaterial minds and material things could causally affect each other. By eliminating immaterial substances, chapter 3 establishes ontological physicalism, the thesis that bits of matter and their aggregates exhaust the content of the world.

Immaterial minds having been banished, the main remaining question concerns the status of mental properties. In chapter 2, it was argued that if mental properties are to retain their causal efficacy, they must be reducible to physical properties. The saving of minds' causal efficacy is widely considered a presumptive (some would say, nonnegotiable) desideratum. However, it is not proper simply to assume the reality of mental causation as a premise and then derive from it the physical reducibility of the mental. The reducibility of mentality must be assessed on its own merit.

Some writers have claimed that although mind-body reduction cannot be carried through, this does not preclude the possibility of *reductive explanation* of the mental in terms of the physical/biological. In chapter 4, I examine reduction, reductive explanation, and their relationship, in general terms as well as in relation to the mind-body case. Reductive explanation of mentality apparently requires the derivation of psychological statements from statements about neural/physical states and processes. How can this be accomplished? There appear to be three presumptive possibilities: (i) via psychoneural correlation laws as auxiliary premises (Nagelian bridge-law reduction); (ii) via conceptual connections between mental properties and physical/behavioral properties (functional reduction); (iii) via a posteriori necessary psychoneural identities as additional premises (identity reduction). It is easily shown that bridge-law reduction does not yield genuine reduction or reductive explanation, and I discuss how (ii) and (iii) might generate reductive explanations, or help close the "explanatory gap." Making use of (ii) requires the functional definability of mental properties in terms of physical/behavioral properties, and (iii) presupposes the availability of psychoneural identities. One side result of this discussion is that reduction and reductive explanation are more intimately tied to each other than sometimes supposed.

In chapter 5, I raise doubts about the availability of psychoneural identities by undermining a currently popular argument for psychoneural type identities, namely the explanatory argument. The claim is that these identities are warranted because of the indispensable role they play in generating explanations of phenomena that would otherwise remain unexplained. The argument comes in two forms. The first begins with the observation that psychoneural correlations are pervasively observed, and that they require explanations. It is then claimed that psychoneural identities (for example, "Pain = C-fiber stimulation") provide the "best" explanation of the correlations ("Pain occurs if and only if C-fibers are stimulated"), and therefore must be accepted. I show that this argument is seriously flawed. The second form of the explanatory argument forgoes the claim that psychoneural identities explain psychoneural correlations; on the contrary, the identities render the demand for explanations of the correlations incoherent and wrongheaded. Rather, we need these identities if we want to bring neurobiological theory to bear on the explanation of psychological facts. Pain causes distress. Why? Because pain is identical with neural state N_1, distress is identical with neural state N_2, and neurophysiology tells us a detailed story about how neural state N_1 causes neural state N_2. The general point is that psychoneural identities can generate neural/physical explanations of psychological regularities, and that this is sufficient warrant for their acceptance. This argument, too, can be seen to be critically flawed. The fundamental problem with both forms of the explanatory arguments concerns the role of identities in explanations. I argue that in explanatory derivations the essential function of identities is to serve as "rewrite" rules (by putting "equals for equals"), and that they are not capable of generating explanatory connections on their own. Thus, both explanatory arguments fail. Moreover, type physicalism has yet to overcome more than a few familiar objections, such as the multiple realization argument and various well-known epistemic arguments. It is plausible to conclude that psychoneural type identities are not going to be available to underwrite an identity reduction of the mind, or to close the explanatory gap.

Chapter 6 begins with a recapitulation of the arguments of the previous chapters, with a view to determining the progress of the overall argument of the book up to this point. The position we have arrived at may be called *conditional physical reductionism*, the thesis that if mental properties are to be causally efficacious, they must be physically reducible. That is, to save mental causation we must reduce mentality. This is the challenge faced by physicalism. With reduction via psychoneural laws and via psychoneural identities having been ruled out, the only remaining reductive option is functional reduction. Considerations are offered in support of the view that cognitive/intentional properties, such as belief, desire, and perception, are functionally characterizable and hence reducible, but that qualia are not so reducible. (A position like this has been advocated by others as well.) According to conditional reductionism, therefore, the causal efficacy of cognitive/intentional states can be vindicated (this saves agency and cognition from epiphenomenalism), but epiphenomenalism still threatens qualia. The battle, however, is not entirely lost for qualia, for some crucial relational properties of qualia—in particular, their similarities and differences—are behaviorally manifest, making their functional characterization possible. Moreover, it is qualia similarities and differences, not their intrinsic qualities, that make a difference to cognition and behavior. The intrinsic qualities of qualia cannot be captured within the physical domain, but that is no great loss. The final conclusion, therefore, is this: Physicalism is not the whole truth, but it is the truth near enough.

I

Mental Causation and Consciousness

OUR TWO MIND-BODY PROBLEMS

SCHOPENHAUER famously called the mind-body problem a *"Weltknoten,"* or "world-knot," and he was surely right. The problem, however, is not really a single problem; it is a cluster of connected problems about the relationship between mind and matter. What these problems are depends on a broader framework of philosophical and scientific assumptions and presumptions within which the questions are posed and possible answers formulated. For the contemporary physicalist, there are two problems that truly make the mind-body problem a *Weltknoten*, an intractable and perhaps ultimately insoluble puzzle. They concern mental causation and consciousness. The problem of mental causation is to answer this question: How can the mind exert its causal powers in a world that is fundamentally physical? The problem of consciousness is to answer the following question: How can there be such a thing as consciousness in a physical world, a world consisting ultimately of nothing but bits of matter distributed over spacetime behaving in accordance with physical law? As it turns out, the two problems are interconnected—the two knots are intertwined, and this makes it all the more difficult to unsnarl either of them.

MENTAL CAUSATION AND CONSCIOUSNESS

Devising an account of mental causation has been, for the past three decades, one of the main preoccupations of philosophers of mind who are committed to physicalism in one form or another. The problem of course is not new: as every student of western philosophy knows, Descartes, who arguably invented the mind-body problem, was forcefully confronted by his contemporaries on this issue.[1] But this does not mean that Descartes's problem is our problem. His problem, as his contemporaries saw it, was to show how his all-too-commonsensical thesis of mind-body interaction was tenable within an ontology of two radically diverse substances, minds and bodies. In his replies, Descartes hemmed and hawed, but in the end was unable to produce an effective response. (In a later chapter we will discuss in some detail the difficulties that mental causation presents to the substance dualist.) It is noteworthy that many of Descartes's peers chose to abandon mental causation rather than the dualism of two substances. Malebranche's occasionalism denies outright that mental causation ever takes place, and Spinoza's double-aspect theory seems to leave no room for genuine causal transactions between mind and matter. Leibniz is well known for having denied causal relations between individual substances altogether, arguing that an illusion of causality arises out of preestablished harmony among the monads. In retrospect, it is more than a little amazing to realize that Descartes was an exception rather than the rule, among the great Rationalists of his day, in defending mental causation as an integral element of his view of the mind. Perhaps most philosophers of this time were perfectly comfortable with the idea that God is the sole causal agent in the entire world, and,

---

1. For Gassendi's vigorous challenge to Descartes, see *The Philosophical Writings of Descartes*, vol. 2, ed. John Cottingham, Robert Stoothoff, and Dugald Murdoch (Cambridge: Cambridge University Press, 1985), p. 238.

with God monopolizing the world's causal power, the epiphenomenalism of human minds just was not something to worry
about. In any case, it is interesting to note that mental causation is regarded with much greater seriousness by us today than
it apparently was by most philosophers in Descartes' time.

In any case, substance dualism is not the source of our current worries about mental causation; substantival minds are no
longer a live option for most of us. What is new and surprising
about the current problem of mental causation is the fact that
it has arisen out of the very heart of physicalism. This means
that giving up the Cartesian conception of minds as immaterial substances in favor of a materialist ontology does not make
the problem go away. On the contrary, our basic physicalist
commitments, as I will argue, can be seen as the source of our
current difficulties.

Let us first review some of the reasons for wanting to save
mental causation—why it is important to us that mental causation is real. First and foremost, the possibility of human agency,
and hence our moral practice, evidently requires that our mental states have causal effects in the physical world. In voluntary
actions our beliefs and desires, or intentions and decisions,
must somehow cause our limbs to move in appropriate ways,
thereby causing the objects around us to be rearranged. That is
how we manage to navigate around the objects in our surroundings, find food and shelter, build bridges and cities, and
destroy the rain forests. Second, the possibility of human
knowledge presupposes the reality of mental causation: perception, our sole window on the world, requires the causation of
perceptual experiences and beliefs by objects and events around
us. Reasoning, by which we acquire new knowledge and belief
from the existing fund of what we already know or believe, involves the causation of new belief by old belief. Memory is a
causal process involving experiences, physical storage of the information contained therein, and its retrieval. If you take away
perception, memory, and reasoning, you pretty much take away

all of human knowledge. Even more broadly, there seem to be compelling reasons for thinking that our capacity to think about and refer to things and phenomena of the world—that is, our capacity for intentionality and speech—depends on our being, or having been, in appropriate cognitive relations with things outside us, and that these cognitive relations essentially involve causal relations. To move on, it seems plain that the possibility of psychology as a science capable of generating law-based explanations of human behavior depends on the reality of mental causation: mental phenomena must be capable of functioning as indispensable links in causal chains leading to physical behavior, like movements of the limbs and vibrations of the vocal cord. A science that invokes mental phenomena in its explanations is presumptively committed to their causal efficacy; if a phenomenon is to have an explanatory role, its presence or absence must make a difference—a *causal* difference. Determinism threatens human agency and skepticism puts human knowledge in peril. The stakes are higher with mental causation, for this problem threatens to take away both agency and cognition.

Let us now briefly turn to consciousness, an aspect of mentality that was oddly absent from both philosophy and scientific psychology for much of the century that has just passed. As everyone knows, consciousness has returned as a major problematic in both philosophy and science, and the last two decades has seen a phenomenal growth and proliferation of research programs and publications on consciousness, not to mention symposia and conferences all over the world.

For most of us, there is no need to belabor the centrality of consciousness to our conception of ourselves as creatures with minds. But I want to point to the ambivalent, almost paradoxical, attitude that philosophers have displayed toward consciousness. As just noted, consciousness had been virtually banished from the philosophical and scientific scene for much of the last century, and consciousness-bashing still goes on in some quarters, with some reputable philosophers arguing that phenomenal consciousness, or "qualia," is a fiction of bad phi-losophy.[2] And there are philosophers and psychologists who, while they recognize phenomenal consciousness as something real, do not believe that a complete science of human behavior, including cognitive psychology and neuroscience, has a place for consciousness, or that there is a need to invoke conscious-ness in an explanatory/predictive theory of cognition and be-havior. Although consciousness research is thriving, much of cognitive science seems still in the grip of what may be called methodological epiphenomenalism.

Contrast this lowly status of consciousness in science and metaphysics with its lofty standing in moral philosophy and value theory. When philosophers discuss the nature of the intrinsic good, or what is worthy of our desire and volition for its own sake, the most prominently mentioned candidates are things like pleasure, absence of pain, enjoyment, and happiness—states that are either states of conscious experience or states that presuppose a capacity for conscious experience. Our attitude toward sentient creatures, with a capacity for pain and pleasure, is crucially different in moral terms from our at-titude toward insentient objects. To most of us, a fulfilling life, a life worth living, is one that is rich and full in qualitative con-sciousness. We would regard a life as impoverished and not fully satisfying if it never included experiences of things like the smell of the sea in a cool morning breeze, the lambent play of sunlight on brilliant autumn foliage, the fragrance of a field of lavender in bloom, and the vibrant, layered soundscape pro-jected by a string quartet. Conversely, a life filled with intense

2. A frequently cited source of consciousness eliminativism is Daniel C. Dennett, "Quining Qualia," in *Consciousness in Contemporary Science*, ed. A. J. Marcel and E. Bisiach (Oxford: Clarendon, 1988). See also Georges Rey, "A Question about Consciousness," in *Perspectives on Mind*, ed. Herbert Otto and James Tuedio (Norwell, MA: Kluwer, 1988). Both are reprinted in *The Nature of Consciousness*, ed. Ned Block, Owen Flanagan, and Güven Güzeldere (Cambridge, MA: MIT Press, 1997).

chronic pains, paralyzing fears and anxieties, an unremitting sense of despair and hopelessness, or a constant monotone depression would strike us as terrible and intolerable, and perhaps not even worth living. In his speech accepting the Nobel Prize in 1904, Ivan Pavlov, whose experiments on animal behavior conditioning probably gave a critical impetus to the behaviorist movement, had this to say: "In point of fact, only one thing in life is of actual interest for us—our psychical experience."[3] It is an ironic fact that the felt qualities of conscious experience, perhaps the only things that ultimately matter to us, are often relegated in the rest of philosophy to the status of "secondary qualities," in the shadowy zone between the real and the unreal, or even jettisoned outright as artifacts of confused minds.

What then is the philosophical problem of consciousness? In *The Principles of Psychology*, published in 1890, William James wrote:

> According to the assumptions of this book, thoughts accompany the brain's workings, and those thoughts are cognitive of realities. The whole relation is one which we can only write down empirically, confessing that no glimmer of explanation of it is yet in sight. That brains should give rise to a knowing consciousness at all, this is the one mystery which returns, no matter of what sort the consciousness and of what sort the knowledge may be. Sensations, aware of mere qualities, involve the mystery as much as thoughts, aware of complex systems, involve it.[4]

In this passage, James is recognizing, first of all, that thoughts and sensations, that is, various modes of mentality and consciousness, arise out of neural processes in the brain. But we can only make a list of, or "write down empirically" as he says, the observed de facto correlations that connect thoughts and

3. Ivan Pavlov, *Experimental Psychology and Other Essays* (New York: Philosophical Library, 1957), p. 148.

4. *The Principles of Psychology* (Cambridge, MA: Harvard University Press, 1981), p. 647; first published in 1890.

sensations to types of neural processes. Making a running list of psychoneural correlations does not come anywhere near gaining an explanatory insight into why there are such correlations; according to James, "no glimmer of explanation" is "yet in sight" as to why these particular correlations hold, or why indeed the brain should give rise to thoughts and consciousness at all.

Why does pain arise when the C-fibers are activated (according to philosophers' fictional neurophysiology), and not under another neural condition? Why doesn't the sensation of itch or tickle arise from C-fiber activation? Why should any conscious experience arise when C-fibers fire? Why should there be something like consciousness in a world that is ultimately nothing but bits of matter scattered over spacetime regions? These questions are precisely the explanatory/ predictive challenges posed by the classic emergentists, like Samuel Alexander, C. Lloyd Morgan, and C. D. Broad— challenges that they despaired of meeting.

These, then, are the problems of mental causation and consciousness. Each of them poses a fundamental challenge to the physicalist worldview. How can the mind exercise its causal powers in a causally closed physical world? Why is there, and how can there be, such a thing as the mind, or consciousness, in a physical world? We will see that these two problems, mental causation and consciousness, are intertwined, and that, in a sense, they make each other insoluble.

I now want to set out in some detail how the problem of mental causation arises within a physicalist setting.

THE SUPERVENIENCE/EXCLUSION ARGUMENT

Mind-body supervenience can usefully be thought of as defining *minimal physicalism*—that is, it is a shared minimum commitment of all positions that are properly called physicalist, though it may not be all that physicalism requires. As is well

known, there are many different ways of formulating a supervenience thesis.[5] For present purposes we will not need an
elaborate statement of exactly what mind-body supervenience
amounts to. It will suffice to understand it as the claim that
what happens in our mental life is wholly dependent on, and
determined by, what happens with our bodily processes. In this
sense, mind-body supervenience is a commitment of all forms
of reductionist physicalism (or type physicalism), such as the
classic Smart-Feigl mind-brain identity thesis.[6] Moreover, it is
also a commitment of functionalism about mentality, arguably
still the orthodoxy on the mind-body problem. Functionalism
views mental properties as defined in terms of their causal roles
in behavioral and physical contexts, and it is evidently committed to the thesis that systems that are alike in intrinsic physical
properties must be alike in respect of their mental or psychological character. The reason is simple: we expect identically
constituted physical systems to be causally indistinguishable in
all physical and behavioral contexts. It is noteworthy that emergentism, too, appears to be committed to supervenience: If two
systems are wholly alike physically, we should expect the same
mental properties to emerge, or fail to emerge, in each; physically indiscernible systems cannot differ in respect of their
emergent properties. Supervenience of emergents in this sense
was explicitly noted and endorsed by C. D. Broad.[7]

5. See Brian McLaughlin, "Varieties of Supervenience," in *Supervenience:
New Essays*, ed. Elias Savellos and Ümit Yalçin (Cambridge: Cambridge University Press, 1995).

6. Herbert Feigl, "The 'Mental' and the 'Physical'," in *Minnesota Studies in
the Philosophy of Science*, vol. 2 (Minneapolis: University of Minnesota Press,
1958); J.J.C. Smart, "Sensations and Brain Processes," *Philosophical Review* 68
(1959): 141–56.

7. C. D. Broad, *The Mind and Its Place in Nature* (London: Routledge and
Kegan Paul, 1925), p. 64. For more details on why supervenience must be an
ingredient of emergence, see my "Being Realistic about Emergence," in *The
Emergence of Emergence*, ed. Paul Davies and Philip Clayton (forthcoming).

Mind-body supervenience has been embraced by some philosophers as an attractive option because it has seemed to them a possible way of protecting the autonomy of the mental domain without lapsing back into antiphysicalist dualism. Just as normative/moral properties are thought to supervene on descriptive/nonmoral properties without being reducible to them, the psychological character of a creature may supervene on and yet remain distinct and autonomous from its physical nature. In many ways, this is an appealing picture: while acknowledging the primacy and priority of the physical domain, it highlights the distinctiveness of creatures with mentality— creatures with consciousness, purposiveness, and rationality. It reaffirms our commonsense belief in our own specialness as beings endowed with intelligent and creative capacities of the kind unseen in the rest of nature. Further, this view provides the burgeoning science of psychology and cognition with a philosophical rationale as an autonomous science in its own right: it investigates these irreducible psychological properties, functions, and capacities, discovering laws and regularities governing them and generating law-based explanations and predictions. It is a science with its own proper domain untouched by other sciences, especially those at the lower levels, like biology, chemistry, and physics.

This seductive picture, however, turns out to be a piece of wishful thinking, when we consider the problem of mental causation—how it is possible, on such a picture, for mentality to have causal powers, powers to influence the course of natural events. Several principles, all of which seem unexceptionable, especially for the physicalist, conspire to make trouble for mental causation. The first of these is the principle that the physical world constitutes a causally closed domain. For our purposes we may state it as follows:

The causal closure of the physical domain. If a physical event has a cause at t, then it has a physical cause at t.

There is also an explanatory analogue of this principle (but we will make no explicit use of it here): If a physical event has a causal explanation (in terms of an event occurring at t), it has a physical causal explanation (in terms of a physical event at t).[8] According to this principle, physics is causally and explanatorily *self-sufficient*: there is no need to go outside the physical domain to find a cause, or a causal explanation, of a physical event. It is plain that physical causal closure is entirely consistent with mind-body dualism and does not beg the question against dualism as such; it does not say that physical events and entities are all that there are in this world, or that physical causation is all the causation that there is. As far as physical causal closure goes, there may well be entities and events outside the physical domain, and causal relations might hold between these nonphysical items. There could even be sciences that investigate these nonphysical things and events. Physical causal closure, therefore, does not rule out mind-body dualism—in fact, not even substance dualism; for all it cares, there might be immaterial souls outside the spacetime physical world. If there were such things, the only constraint that the closure principle lays down is that they not causally meddle with physical events—that is, there can be no causal influences injected into the physical domain from outside. Descartes's interactionist dualism, therefore, is precluded by physical causal closure; however, Leibniz's doctrine of preestablished harmony and mind-body parallelism, like Spinoza's double-aspect theory,[9] are perfectly consistent with it. Notice that neither the mental nor the biological domain is causally closed; there are mental

8. The closure principle should be distinguished from the thesis of physical determinism to the effect that every physical event has a physical cause. Physical causal closure should make sense even if some physical events don't have causes.

9. Here I am referring to the bare mind-body ontologies associated with Leibniz and Spinoza; I rather doubt that Leibniz's metaphysics of monads or Spinoza's metaphysics with God as the only substance would allow real causal relations even within the physical domain.

and biological events whose causes are not themselves mental or biological events. A trauma to the head can cause the loss of consciousness and exposure to intense radiation can cause cells to mutate.

Moreover, physical causal closure does not by itself exclude nonphysical causes, or causal explanations, of physical events. As we will see, however, such causes and explanations could be ruled out when an exclusion principle like the following is adopted:

> *Principle of causal exclusion.* If an event *e* has a sufficient cause *c* at *t*, no event at *t* distinct from *c* can be a cause of *e* (unless this is a genuine case of causal overdetermination).

There is also a companion principle regarding causal explanation, that is, the principle of explanatory exclusion, but we will not need it for present purposes. Note that the exclusion principle as stated is a general metaphysical principle and does not refer specifically to mental or physical causes; in particular, it does not favor physical causes over mental causes. It is entirely neutral as between the mental and the physical. For our purposes, it will be convenient to have on hand a generalized version of the exclusion principle.

> *Principle of determinative/generative exclusion.* If the occurrence of an event *e*, or an instantiation of a property P, is determined/generated by an event *c*—causally or otherwise—then *e*'s occurrence is not determined/generated by any event wholly distinct from or independent of *c*—unless this is a genuine case of overdetermination.[10]

The second principle broadens causation, or causal determination, to generation/determination simpliciter, whether causal or of another kind. The intuitive idea is the idea of an event or

---

10. In chapter 2 this broader principle will be dispensed with in formulating the supervenience argument.

state, or a property instantiation, owing its existence to another event or state—or, to put another way, the idea that one
thing is generated out of, or derives its existence from, another.
What I have in mind is very close to the fundamental notion of
causation, or determination, that I believe Elizabeth Anscombe
was after in her *Causality and Determination.*[11] Causation as
generation, or effective production and determination, is in
many ways a stronger relation than mere counterfactual dependence,[12] and it is causation in this sense that is fundamentally involved in the problem of mental causation. Another
way in which a state, or property instance, is generated is
supervenience; the aesthetic properties of a work of art are
generated in the sense I have in mind by its physical properties. So are moral properties of acts and persons generated by
their nonmoral, descriptive properties. It is the relation that
sanctions the assertion that something has a certain property
because, or *in virtue of* the fact that, it has certain other properties that generate it. I have argued elsewhere for the causal/
explanatory exclusion principle;[13] I believe that the fundamental rationale for the broader principle is essentially the same,
and that anyone who finds the former plausible should find the
latter equally plausible.

It is quick and easy to see how these principles create trou-
bles for mental causation for anyone who accepts mind-body

11. Cambridge: Cambridge University Press, 1971. Reprinted in *Causation*,
ed. Ernest Sosa and Michael Tooley (Oxford: Oxford University Press, 1993).

12. It is in some respects weaker than counterfactual dependence; in cases
of preemption and overdetermination, generative causation may hold without
counterfactual dependence. The two notions are not strictly comparable, and
that is why the counterfactual accounts of causation continue to have difficulties with preemption and overdetermination, showing, in my opinion, that our
core idea of causation is more intimately tied to generative/productive causation than to counterfactual dependence.

13. See, e.g., "Mechanism, Purpose, and Explanatory Exclusion," reprinted
in my *Supervenience and Mind* (Cambridge: Cambridge University Press,
1993); first published in 1989.

supervenience—that is, for anyone who is a minimal physical-ist. I have called the line of considerations to be presented below "the supervenience argument"; in the literature, it is also known as "the exclusion argument." (For usage uniformity, it is best to think of the supervenience argument as a special form of the exclusion argument, and take the latter as a generic form of argument with the conclusion that mental cause is always excluded by physical cause.) Briefly, the argument goes like this.[14] Suppose that an instantiation of mental property M causes another mental property, M*, to instantiate. (We take property instantiations as events; instantiations of a mental property are mental events, and similarly for physical properties and physical events.) This is perfectly consistent with physical causal closure. But mind-body supervenience says that this instantiation of mental property M* occurs in virtue of the fact that one of the physical properties on which M* supervenes is instantiated at that time; call this physical base property P*. This means that given that P* is instantiated on this occasion, M* must of necessity be instantiated on this occasion. That is, the M*-instance is wholly dependent on, and is generated by, the P*-instance. At this point, the exclusion principle kicks in: Is the occurrence of the M*-instance due to its supposed cause, the M-instance, or its supervenience base event, P*-instance? It must be one or the other, but which one? Given that its physical supervenience base P* is instantiated on this occasion, M* must be instantiated as well on this occasion, regardless of what might have preceded this M*-instance. In what sense, then, can the M-instance be said to be a "cause," or a generative source, of the M*-instance?

14. This argument will be discussed in greater detail in chapter 2, including responses to some of the objections and criticisms that have been raised against it. I first presented this argument in an explicit form in "'Downward Causation' in Emergentism and Nonreductive Materialism," in *Emergence or Reduction?*, ed. Ansgar Beckermann, Hans Flohr, and Jaegwon Kim (Berlin: De Gruyter, 1992).

I believe that the only acceptable way of reconciling the two causal/generative claims and achieving a consistent picture of the situation is this: the M*-instance caused the M*-instance *by causing* the P*-instance. More generally, the following principle seems highly plausible: *In order to cause a supervenient property to be instantiated, you must cause one of its base properties to be instantiated.* In order to alter the aesthetic properties of a work of art, you must alter the physical properties on which the aesthetic properties supervene; in order to do something about your headache you must causally intervene in the brain state on which the headache, supervenes. There is no other way; this is what makes the idea of telepathy (for example, a thought of mine directly causing a thought in you) not credible if not incoherent—unless of course one could telepathically influence another person's brain processes. (In fact, for present purposes, this principle concerning the causation of supervenient properties, which I believe is independently plausible, can replace the principle of determinative/generative exclusion, which some might find too broad.)

So M causes M* to instantiate by causing P* to instantiate, from which it trivially follows that the M-instance causes a P*-instance. But this is a case of mental-to-physical causation. Turning our attention now to the supposed mental cause M, we see that, by mind-body supervenience, M must have its own physical supervenience base; call it P. When we consider the total picture, there seems every reason to consider P to be a cause of P*. If we think of causation in terms of sufficiency, P is clearly sufficient for P*, since it is sufficient for M and M is sufficient for P*. If we think of causation in terms of counterfactuals, we may assume that if P had not been there, the supervening M wouldn't have been there either, and that since M is what brought about P*, P* wouldn't be there either. So at this point we have the following two causal claims: M causes P*, and P causes P*.

Now, given psychophysical property dualism espoused by the nonreductive physicalist, M and P are distinct properties.

This means that P* has two causes each sufficient for it and occurring at the same time (a supervenient property and its base properties are always instantiated at the same time). At this point the causal exclusion principle applies: either M or P must be disqualified as P*'s cause. A moment's reflection shows that it is M that must be disqualified. The reason is that if P is disqualified, the causal closure principle kicks in again, saying that since a physical event, P*, has a cause (namely M), it must have a physical cause (occurring at the same time as M)—the disqualified P will do—and we are back in the same situation, a situation in which we again have to choose between a physical and a mental cause. Unless mental cause M is jettisoned in favor of P, we would be off to an infinite regress—or be forever treading water in the same place.

The final picture that has emerged is this: P is a cause of P*, with M and M* supervening respectively on P and P*. There is a single underlying causal process in this picture, and this process connects two physical properties, P and P*. The correlations between M and M* and between M and P* are by no means accidental or coincidental; they are lawful and counterfactual-sustaining regularities arising out of M's and M*'s supervenience on the causally linked P and P*. These observed correlations give us an impression of causation; however, that is only an appearance, and there is no more causation here than between two successive shadows cast by a moving car, or two successive symptoms of a developing pathology. This is a simple and elegant picture, metaphysically speaking, but it will prompt howls of protest from those who think that it has given away something very special and precious, namely the causal efficacy of our minds. Thus is born the problem of mental causation.

The problem of mental causation. Causal efficacy of mental properties is inconsistent with the joint acceptance of the following four claims: (i) physical causal closure, (ii) causal exclusion,

(iii) mind-body supervenience, and (iv) mental/physical property dualism—the view that mental properties are irreducible
to physical properties.

Physical causal closure and mind-body supervenience are, or
should be, among the shared commitments of all physicalists.
The exclusion principles are general metaphysical constraints,
and I don't see how they can be successfully challenged. This
leaves mind-body property dualism as the only negotiable
item. But to negotiate it away is to embrace reductionism.
This will cause a chill in those physicalists who want to eat the
cake and have it too—that is, those who want both the irreducibility and causal efficacy of the mental. I believe that the
question no longer is whether or not those of us who want
to protect mental causation find mind-body reductionism
palatable. What has become increasingly clear after three
decades of debate is that if we want robust mental causation,
we had better be prepared to take reductionism seriously,
whether we like it or not. But even if you are ready for reductionism, it doesn't necessarily mean that you can have it. For
reductionism may not be true. This is the point to which we
now turn.

Can We Reduce Qualia? conscious experience

Before reduction and reductionism can be usefully discussed,
we need to be tolerably clear about the model of reduction appropriate to the issues on hand. I believe much of the philosophical debate during the past few decades concerning the
reducibility of the mental has turned out to be a futile exercise
because it was predicated on the wrong model of reduction. This
is the derivational model of intertheoretic reduction developed
by Ernest Nagel in the 1950s and '60s. As is widely known, the
heart of Nagel reduction is *bridge laws*, the empirical lawlike
principles that are supposed to connect the properties of the
domain to be reduced with the properties of the base domain.

reductionism → people are atoms, physical states

Specifically, the requirement, as standardly understood, is that each property up for reduction be connected by a bridge law with a nomologically coextensive property in the base domain. Most of the influential antireductionist arguments—notably, Davidson's anomalist argument and the Putnam-Fodor multiple realization argument[15]—have focused on showing that the bridge law requirement cannot be met for mental properties in relation to physical/biological properties.

All this is by now a familiar story, and there is no need here to rehearse the arguments, counterarguments, and so forth. But the philosophical emptiness of Nagel reduction is quickly seen when we notice that a Nagel reduction of the mental to the physical is consistent with, and even in some cases entailed by, many all-out dualisms, such as the double-aspect theory, the doctrine of preestablished harmony, epiphenomenalism, and even emergentism. The reason of course is that these dualisms are consistent with the mind-body bridge law requirement; in fact, some of them, like the double-aspect theory, entail the satisfaction of this requirement. This objection can be circumvented by strengthening the bridge laws into identities— that is, by requiring the bridging principles connecting the reducing and reduced theories to take the form of an identity ("pain = C-fiber activation") rather than a biconditional law ("pain occurs to an organism at a time just in case its C-fibers are activated at that time")—that is, by moving from bridge-law reduction to identity reduction.[16] It has recently

15. Donald Davidson, "Mental Events," reprinted in his *Essays on Actions and Events* (Oxford and New York: Oxford University Press, 1980); first published in 1970. Hilary Putnam, "The Nature of Mental States," in his *Philosophical Papers*, vol. 2 (Cambridge: Cambridge University Press, 1975); first published in 1967. Jerry A. Fodor, "Special Sciences—or the Disunity of Science as a Working Hypothesis," *Synthese* 27 (1974): 97–115.

16. As early as the 1970s Robert L. Causey argued that microreduction requires cross-level identities of properties, and that genuine reductions cannot be based merely on bridge laws affirming property correlations; see his "Attribute-Identities in Microreductions," *Journal of Philosophy* 69 (1972): 407–422.

been suggested that an identity reduction of consciousness is just what is needed to close the much-discussed "explanatory gap" between the brain and conscious experience. We will look at the feasibility of identity reduction for consciousness in later chapters (chapters 4 and 5). The main problem with this proposal, as we will see, concerns the availability of mind-body identities for reductive purposes. I will argue that the principal arguments advanced for psychoneural identities, namely that they serve certain essential explanatory purposes, do not work, and that there is no visible reason to think that such identities are true or that we will ever be entitled to them.

What then is required to reduce a mental property, say pain? I believe that what has to be done is, first, to *functionalize* pain (or, more precisely, the property of being in pain): namely, to show that being in pain is definable as being in a state (or instantiating a property) that is caused by certain inputs (i.e., tissue damage, trauma) and that in turn causes certain behavioral and other outputs (i.e., characteristic pain behaviors, a sense of distress, a desire to be rid of it). More generally, instantiating a mental property M, upon M's functionalization, will turn out to be being in some state or other that is typically caused by a certain specified set of stimulus conditions and that in turn typically causes a certain specified set of outputs. Next, once a mental property has been functionalized, we can look for its "realizers"—that is, states or properties that satisfy the causal specification defining that mental property. Thus, for pain, we look for an internal state in an organism that is caused to instantiate by tissue damage and trauma and whose instantiation in turn causes characteristic pain behaviors (and possibly outputs of other kinds). In the case of humans and perhaps mammals in general, the state turns out to be, let us say, electrical activity in a certain cortical zone—call it Q. That is, neural state Q is the realizer of pain for humans and mammals. Conventional wisdom has it that pain and other mental states have multiple diverse realizers across different species and structures, and perhaps even among members of the same species (or even in the same individual over time). This means that this second step of finding realizers of a mental property is likely to be an ongoing affair with no clear end. Obviously, we are not going to find, nor would we necessarily be interested in identifying, all actual and possible realizers of pain for all actual and possible pain-capable organisms and systems. Functional reduction, as I call it, can focus on the reduction of a mental property, or a group of them, for a specific population—that is, neural research on pain will aim at *local* reductions, not a one-shot *global* reduction (as suggested by the Nagel bridge-law model). We may be interested in finding the neural basis of human pain, or canine pain, or Martian pain. We may be interested in identifying the neural basis of your pain now or my pain yesterday. Neural bases may differ for different instances of pain, but individual pains must nonetheless reduce to their respective neural/physical realizers. Unlike in the case of Nagelian bridge-law reduction, the multiple realizability of pain is no barrier to local reduction by functionalization. Suppose that pain has physical realizers, P_1, P_2, ... Then, any given instance of pain is an instance of either P_1 or of P_2 or . . . . If you are in pain in virtue of being in state P_k, there is nothing more, or less, to your being in pain than your being in state P_k. This particular pain is the very same state as this instance of P_k. Each pain instance is a P_1-instance, or P_2-instance, or . . . ; that is, all pain instances reduce to the instances of its realizers.[17]

If pain can be functionalized in this sense, its instances will have the causal powers of pain's realizers. Thus, if a given

17. See my "Making Sense of Emergence," *Philosophical Studies* 95 (1999): 3–36, and *Mind in a Physical World* (Cambridge, MA: MIT Press, 1998) for more details, in particular concerning how reductions conforming to this model meet the basic methodological and metaphysical requirements of reduction. More details on functional reduction can be found in chapter 4 below.

instance of pain occurs in virtue of the instantiation of physical realizer P_k, that pain instance has the causal powers of this instance of P_k. This will solve the problem of the causal efficacy of pains—that is, provided that pain can be functionalized. It is important to see that this result cannot be achieved by simply assuming that P_k is a *neural correlate*, or *substrate*, of pain. It might be that pain and P_k correlate with each other because they are both the effects of a common cause; if such is the case there obviously is no reason for thinking that a given occurrence of pain and the corresponding instance of P_k have the same causal powers, or that they are one and the same event. Pain and its realizers are much more intimately related: to be in pain is to be in a state meeting causal specification C—that is, to be in pain *is* to instantiate one of its realizers—and if you are in pain in virtue of instantiating pain-realizer P_k, there is no pain event over and above this instantiation of P_k.

So if pain is functionalized, the problem of mental causation has a simple solution for all pain instances. But what of the causal efficacy of pain itself? What should we say about the causal powers of pain as a mental kind? The answer is that as a kind pain will be causally heterogeneous, as heterogeneous as the heterogeneity of its diverse realizers. Pain, as a kind, will lack the kind of causal/nomological unity we expect of true natural kinds, kinds in terms of which scientific theorizing is conducted. This is what we must expect given that pain is a functional property with multiple diverse physical realizers. If the term "multiple" in "multiple realizations" means anything, it must mean causal/nomological multiplicity; if two realizers of pain are not causally or nomologically diverse, there is no reason to count them as two, not one. On this reductive account, pain will not be causally impotent or epiphenomenal; it is only that pain is causally heterogeneous.

The key question then is this: Is pain functionally reducible? Are mental properties in general functionalizable and hence functionally reducible? Or are they "emergent" and irreducible? I believe that there is reason to think that intentional/cognitive properties are functionalizable. However, I am with those who believe that phenomenal properties of consciousness are not functional properties. To argue for this view of phenomenal properties, or qualia, we do not need anything as esoteric and controversial as the "zombie" hypothesis much discussed recently[18]—that is, the claim that zombies, creatures that are indiscernible from us physically and behaviorally but who lack consciousness, are metaphysically possible. All we need is something considerably more modest, namely the metaphysical possibility of qualia inversion. Perhaps the problem is still open, but I believe there are substantial and weighty reasons, and a sufficiently broad consensus among the philosophers who work in this area,[19] to believe that qualia are functionally irreducible.

Moreover, it is easily seen that if qualia are functionally reducible, the problem posed by James and others about consciousness can be solved. Suppose that pain has been functionalized and its realizer identified for humans. Consider a functional characterization of pain like this: To be in pain is to be in a state that is caused by tissue damage and that in turn causes winces and groans. And assume that the venerable C-fiber stimulation is the neural realizer of pain in humans. Consider now the question: Why is Jones in pain at t? Can we derive the statement "Jones is in pain at t" from information exclusively about Jones's physical/behavioral properties (along with other strictly physical/behavioral information)? Given the functional

18. See David Chalmers, *The Conscious Mind* (Oxford and New York: Oxford University Press, 1996).

19. To mention a few: Ned Block, Christopher Hill, Frank Jackson, Joseph Levine, Colin McGinn, and Brian McLaughlin. Issues mentioned in this paragraph will be discussed in greater detail in the chapters to follow.

reduction, the answer is yes, as is shown by the following deduction:

1) Jones's C-fibers are stimulated at t.

2) C-fiber stimulation (in humans) is caused by tissue damage and it in turn causes winces and groans.

3) To be in pain, by definition, is to be in a state which is caused by tissue damage and which in turn causes winces and groans.

4) Therefore, Jones is in pain at t.

Notice that the third line, a functional definition of pain, does not represent empirical/factual information about pain; if anything, it gives us information about the concept pain, or the meaning of "pain." Formally, definitions do not count as premises of a proof; they come free. Notice, moreover, that the displayed derivation could also serve as a prediction of Jones's pain from physical/behavioral information alone. And we could easily convert it into an explanation of why (in humans) pain correlates with C-fiber stimulation, not with another neural state.[20] This derivation would, therefore, answer William James's question why sensations "accompany the brain's workings," a question for which he saw "no glimmer of an explanation." Functional reduction of pain and other sensations would deliver the explanation James was seeking. The only problem is that sensations, or qualia, resist functional reduction, and, as James says, there still is no glimmer of an explanation. But we have made some progress: we now know what is needed to achieve such an explanation.

As earlier noted, there are those who think that functional reduction is not the only way to solve the problem of consciousness; they argue that although pain and other qualia may not be functionally reducible, they are reducible in another way,

20. These issues will be discussed in more detail in chapter 4.

through their identification with physical/neural properties, and that this will enable us to close the gap between consciousness and the brain and thereby provide us with an answer to James's question. We will see in later chapters why this new mind-brain identity reduction is not an option for us. As we will argue,[21] if functional reduction doesn't work for qualia, nothing will.

THE TWO WORLD-KNOTS

Let us take stock of where we are: the problem of mental causation is solvable for a given class of mental properties if and only if these properties are functionally reducible with physical/biological properties as their realizers. But phenomenal mental properties are not functionally definable and hence functionally irreducible. Hence, the problem of mental causation is not solvable for phenomenal mental properties.

But, as we also saw, the problem of consciousness, or "the mystery of consciousness," is solvable if consciousness is functionally reducible—and I will argue that it is solvable *only* if consciousness is functionally reducible. So the functional irreducibility of consciousness entails the unsolvability of both the problem of consciousness and the problem of mental causation—at least as the latter problem concerns consciousness. It is thus that the two problems, that of mental causation and that of consciousness, turn out to share an interlocking fate. What stands in the way of solving the problem of mental causation is consciousness. And what stands in the way of solving the problem of consciousness is the impossibility of interpreting or defining it in terms of its causal relations to physical/biological properties. They are indeed *Weltknoten*, problems that have eluded our best philosophical efforts. They seem deeply

21. In chapters 4 and 5.

entrenched in the way we conceptualize the world and ourselves, and seem to arise from some of the fundamental assumptions we hold about each.

Does this mean that there is some hidden flaw somewhere in our system of concepts and assumptions, and that we need to alter, in some basic way, our conceptual framework to rid ourselves of these problems? Of course, if our scheme of concepts were radically altered, the problems would be altered as well; perhaps, the new scheme would not even permit these, or equivalent, problems to be formulated. Some philosophers would be willing to take this as a sufficient ground for urging us to abandon our present system of concepts in favor of a cleansed and tidier one, claiming that the conundrum of mental causation and consciousness is reason enough for jettisoning our shared scheme of intentional and phenomenal idioms, with its alleged built-in "Cartesian" errors and confusions. There are others who blame our penchant for thinking in terms of robust productive causality for the vexing problem of mental causation. Blaming our system of concepts, or our language, for philosophical difficulties is a familiar philosophical strategy of long standing. To me, this often turns out to be an ostrich strategy—trying to avoid problems by ignoring them. To motivate the discarding of a framework, we need independent reasons—we should be able to show it to be deficient, incomplete, or flawed in some fundamental way, independently of the fact that it generates puzzles and problems that we are unable to deal with. Why should we suppose that all problems are solvable—and solvable by us? (Just because we find difficult, perhaps insoluble, moral problems and puzzles, should we cast aside moral concepts and moral discourse?) It may well be that our mind-body problem, or something close to it, arises within any scheme that is rich enough to do justice to the world as we experience it. It may well be that the problem is an inexorable consequence of the tension between the objective world of physical existence and the subjective world of experience, and that the distinction between the objective and the subjective is unavoidable for reflective cognizers and agents of the kind that we are.[22]

To conclude, then, the mind-body problem, for us, the would-be physicalists, has come down to two problems, mental causation and consciousness, and these together represent the most profound challenge to physicalism. If physicalism is to survive as a worldview for us, it must show just where we belong in the physical world, and this means that it must give an account of our status as conscious creatures with powers to affect our surroundings in virtue of our consciousness and mentality. The arguments that have been presented here already suggest that physicalism will not be able to survive intact and in its entirety. We will try to determine how much of it can survive, and we will see, I hope, that what does survive is good enough for us.

22. A thought like this is suggested by Thomas Nagel in *The View from Nowhere* (New York: Oxford University Press, 1986).

2

The Supervenience Argument
Motivated, Clarified,
and Defended

AN ARGUMENT was presented in the preceding chapter to show that, on an influential position on the mind-body problem, mental properties turn out to be without causal efficacy. This is what I have called the supervenience argument, also called the exclusion argument in the literature. The argument has drawn comments, criticisms, and objections from a wide range of philosophers, but mostly from those who want to defend orthodox nonreductive physicalism and other forms of mind-body property dualism. Critics of the argument have raised some significant issues, both about the specifics of the argument and, more interestingly, about the broader philosophical issues involved. In this chapter, I would like to address two of the more pressing problems. One is that of "overdetermination," brought up by a number of philosophers; the second is the problem of "causal drainage," forcefully developed by Ned Block in his "Do Causal Powers Drain Away?"[1] Before we get to these and other issues, I want to set out the leading idea that motivates the supervenience argument and then offer what

1. Ned Block, "Do Causal Powers Drain Away?" *Philosophy and Phenomenological Research* 67 (2003): 133–150.

I hope will be a clearer statement of the argument, along with explanatory comments that some may find useful. But first we need a brief description of the philosophical position that is the target of the supervenience argument.

Nonreductive Physicalism

There is no consensus on exactly how nonreductive physicalism is to be formulated, for the simple reason that there is no consensus about either how physicalism is to be formulated or how we should understand reduction. For present purposes, however, no precise formulation is needed; a broad-brush characterization will be sufficient. Moreover, there need not be a single "correct" or "right" formulation of physicalism; there probably are a number of claims, not strictly equivalent, about the fundamentally physical character of the world, each of which can reasonably be considered a statement of physicalism. The strengths and weaknesses, merits and demerits, of these different physicalisms could be examined and debated, and reasonable people could come to different conclusions about them. In any case, most will agree that the following three doctrines are central to nonreductive physicalism: mind-body supervenience, the physical irreducibility of the mental, and the causal efficaciousness of the mental. Mind-body supervenience, the claim that makes the position a form of physicalism, can be stated as follows:

> *Supervenience.* Mental properties strongly supervene on physical/biological properties. That is, if any system s instantiates a mental property M at t, there necessarily exists a physical property P such that s instantiates P at t, and necessarily anything instantiating P at any time instantiates M at that time.[2]

2. There are alternative, not quite equivalent, ways of stating mind-body supervenience; one could get a good idea of what these might be from Brian McLaughlin, "Varieties of Supervenience," in *Supervenience: New Essays*, ed. Elias

I take supervenience as an ontological thesis involving the idea of dependence—a sense of dependence that justifies saying that a mental property is instantiated in a given organism at a time *because*, or *in virtue of* the fact that, one of its physical "base" properties is instantiated by the organism at that time. *Supervenience*, therefore, is not a mere claim of covariation between mental and physical properties; it includes a claim of existential dependence of the mental on the physical. I am assuming that a serious physicalist will accept this interpretation of supervenience. Mind-body supervenience as a bare claim about how mental and physical properties covary will be accepted by the double-aspect theorist, the neutral monist, the emergentist, and the epiphenomenalist; it can be accepted even by the substance dualist.

The second component of nonreductive physicalism reflects the "nonreductive" character of this form of physicalism:

> *Irreducibility.* Mental properties are not reducible to, and are not identical with, physical properties.

There is no single well-defined sense, or model, of reduction shared by all disputants in this debate, but this will not matter for us in the context of the supervenience argument; all we need to assume here is that physically irreducible properties remain outside the physical domain—that is, if anything is physically reduced, it must be identical with some physical item. The root meaning of reduction was given, I believe, by J.J.C. Smart when he said that sensations are nothing "over and above" brain processes.[3] If Xs are reduced to Ys, then Xs are nothing over and above the Ys.

Savellos and Ümit Yalçin (Cambridge: Cambridge University Press, 1995). In some contexts the interpretation of "necessarily" as it occurs in the last clause can be crucial; for our purposes, there is no need to opt for any special specification.

3. J.J.C. Smart, "Sensations and Brain Processes," in *The Nature of Mind*, ed. David M. Rosenthal (New York and Oxford: Oxford University Press, 1991), p. 170. Originally published in *Philosophical Review* 68 (1959): 141–56.

We now come to the third doctrine, concerning the causal status of these irreducible mental properties.

Causal efficacy. Mental properties have causal efficacy—that is, their instantiations can, and do, cause other properties, both mental and physical, to be instantiated.

This last thesis is important to the many friends of the position I am describing. The irreducibility claim is often motivated by a desire to save mental properties as something special and distinctive, but if these properties turn out to be causally impotent and explanatorily useless, that would rob them of any real interest or significance, rendering the issue of their reducibility largely moot. Or one could argue that since physical properties are assumed to be causally efficacious, causally inert mental properties obviously cannot be physically reduced. This means that the rejection of mental causal efficacy would make the irreducibility claim true but trivial. In these ways, therefore, the doctrines of irreducibility and causal efficacy go hand in hand.

It can be debated whether these three doctrines constitute a robust enough physicalism. The issue obviously turns on the question whether mind-body supervenience as stated is sufficient for physicalism, since the irreducibility and mental causal efficacy have nothing specifically to do with physicalism; Descartes endorsed both. Moreover, classic emergentism, not usually considered a form of physicalism, endorsed all three, making it a target of the supervenience argument.[4] However, this issue will not affect the discussions to follow. My claims and arguments are intended to apply to any position that accepts the three propositions; what else it accepts makes no difference.

---

4. See my "Being Realistic about Emergence" in *The Emergence of Emergence*, ed. Paul Davies and Philip Clayton (Oxford: Oxford University Press, forthcoming). The three doctrines, however, can be thought of as capturing the physicalist core of emergentism. On supervenience and physicalism, see Jessica Wilson, "Supervenience-Based Formulations of Physicalism," forthcoming in *Noûs*.

The Fundamental Idea

The idea that drives the supervenience argument can be expressed in the following proposition, which I name after the great eighteenth-century American theologian-philosopher Jonathan Edwards:

> *Edwards's dictum.* There is a tension between "vertical" determination and "horizontal" causation. In fact, vertical determination excludes horizontal causation.

What do I mean by "vertical" determination? Consider an object, say this lump of bronze. At any given time it has a variety of intrinsic properties, like color, shape, texture, density, hardness, electrical conductivity, and so on. Most of us would accept the proposition that the bronze has these properties at this time in virtue of the fact that it has, at this time, a certain microstructure—that is, it is composed of molecules of certain kinds (copper and tin) in a certain specific structural configuration. I describe this situation by saying that the macroproperties of the bronze are vertically determined by its synchronous microstructure. The term "vertical" is meant to reflect the usual practice of picturing micro-macro levels in a vertical array, with the micro underpinning the macro. In contrast, we usually represent diachronic causal relations on a horizontal line, from past (left) to future (right)—"time's arrow" seems always to fly from left to right. From the causal point of view, the piece of bronze has the properties it has at t because it had the properties it had at $t - \Delta t$ (and certain boundary conditions obtained during this period). The past determines the future and the future depends on the past. That is what I mean by "horizontal" causation. So we have here two purported determinative relationships orthogonal to each other: vertical micro-macro mereological determination and horizontal past-to-future causal determination.

The lump of bronze has the color yellow at time t. Why is it yellow at t? There are two presumptive answers: (1) because its surface has microstructural property M at t; (2) because it was yellow at $t - \Delta t$. To appreciate the force of the supervenience argument it is essential to see a prima facie tension between these two explanations. As long as the lump has microproperty M at t, it's going to be yellow at t, *no matter what happened before* t. Moreover, unless the lump has M, or another appropriate microproperty (with the right reflectance characteristic), at t, it cannot be yellow at t. Anything that happened before t seems irrelevant to the lump's being yellow at t; its having M at t is fully sufficient in itself to make it yellow at t.

So far as I know, Jonathan Edwards was the first philosopher who saw a tension of precisely this kind. Edwards' surprising doctrine that there are no temporally persisting objects was based on his belief that the existence of such objects is excluded by the fact that God is the sustaining cause of the created world at every instant of time. There are no persisting things because at every moment God creates, or recreates, the entire world *ex nihilo*—that is what it means to say that God is the sustaining cause of the world. Consider two successive "time slices" of the bronze: each slice is created by God, and there is no causal or other direct existential relationship between them. To illustrate his argument, Edwards offers a marvelously apt analogy:

> The *images* of things in a glass, as we keep our eye upon them, seem to remain precisely the same, with a continuing, perfect identity. But it is known to be otherwise. Philosophers well know that these images are constantly renewed, by the impression and reflection of *new* rays of light; so that the image impressed by the former rays is constantly vanishing, and a *new* image is impressed by *new* rays every moment, both on the glass and on the eye.... And the new images being put on *immediately* or *instantly* do not make them the same, any more than if it were done with the intermission of an *hour* or a *day*. The image that exists at this moment is not at all *derived* from the image which existed at the last preceding moment. As may

be seen, because if the succession of new *rays* be intercepted, by
something interposed between the object and the glass, the
image immediately ceases; the *past existence* of the image has no
influence to uphold it, so much as for a moment.[5]

Successive images are not causally related to each other; they
are each caused by something else. If we suppose that the persistence of an object requires causal relations between its earlier
and later stages, Edwards is arguing that "horizontal" causation
involving created substances is excluded by their "vertical" dependence on God as a sustaining cause of the world at every
instant. Remove God as the sustaining cause; the whole world
will vanish at that very instant.[6]

It is simple to see how Edwards's dictum applies to the mind-
body case, causing trouble for mental causation. Mind-body
supervenience, or the idea that the mental is physically
"realized"—in fact, any serious doctrine of mind-body dependence will do—plays the role of vertical determination or
dependence, and mental causation, or any "higher-level" causation, is the horizontal causation at issue. The tension between
vertical determination and horizontal causation, or the former's
threat to preempt and void the latter, has been, at least for me,
at the heart of the worries about mental causation.

---

5. Jonathan Edwards, *Doctrines of Original Sin Defended* (1758), Part IV,
Chapter II. The quotation is from *Jonathan Edwards*, ed. C. H. Faust and
T. H. Johnson (New York: American Book Co., 1935), p. 335. (Italics in the
original.) It seems, however, that Edwards's argument may well have been
foreshadowed by the occasionalists of the 17th century.

6. Some will argue that these considerations—and some of the crucial steps
in the supervenience argument—depend on the use of a robust, "thick" concept of productive or generative causation rather than a "thin" concept based
on the idea of counterfactual dependence or simple Humean "constant conjunctions," and that thin causation is all the causation that there is. See Barry
Loewer's "Comments on Jaegwon Kim's *Mind in a Physical World*," *Philosophy
and Phenomenological Research* 65 (2002): 655–62, and my reply to Loewer,
ibid., 674–77.

THE SUPERVENIENCE ARGUMENT REFINED
AND CLARIFIED

Let us now turn to a restatement of the supervenience argument in a more explicit and streamlined form. It is useful to divide the argument into two stages; I believe each stage has its own interest, and this will also enable me to present two materially different ways of completing the second stage of the argument.

Stage 1

We begin with the supposition that there are cases of mental-to-mental causation. Let M and M* be mental properties:

(1) M causes M*.

Properties as such don't enter into causal relations; when we say "M causes M*," that is short for "An instance of M causes an instance of M*" or "An instantiation of M causes M* to instantiate on that occasion." Also for brevity we suppress reference to times. From *Supervenience*, we have:

(2) For some physical property P*; M* has P*
      as its supervenience base.

As earlier noted, (1) and (2) together give rise to a tension when we consider the question "Why is M* instantiated on this occasion? What is responsible for, and explains, the fact that M* occurs on this occasion?" For there are two seemingly exclusionary answers: (a) "Because M caused M* to instantiate on this occasion," and (b) "Because P*, a supervenience base of M*, is instantiated on this occasion." This of course is where Jonathan Edwards's insight, encapsulated in Edwards's dictum, comes into play: Given that P* is present on this occasion, M* would be there no matter what happened before; as M*'s supervenience base, the instantiation of P* at t in and of itself necessitates M*'s occurrence at *t*. This would be true even if M*'s putative cause, M, had not occurred—*unless, that is, the occurrence of M had something to do with the occurrence of P* on this occasion*. This last observation points to a simple and natural way of dissipating the tension created by (a) and (b):

(3) M caused M* *by* causing its supervenience base P*.

This completes Stage 1. What the argument has shown at this point is that if *Supervenience* is assumed, mental-to-mental causation entails mental-to-physical causation—or, more generally, that "same-level" causation entails "downward" causation. Given *Supervenience*, it is not possible to have causation in the mental realm without causation that crosses into the physical realm. This result is of some significance; if we accept, as most do, some doctrine of macro-micro supervenience, we can no longer isolate causal relations within levels; any causal relation at level L (higher than the bottom level) entails a cross-level, L to L − 1, causal relation. In short, *level-bound causal autonomy is inconsistent with supervenience or dependence between the levels*. Further, an important part of the interest of the supervenience argument is that it shows that, under the physicalist assumptions we are working with, mind-to-mind causation is in trouble just as much as mind-to-body causation. Often the problem of mental causation is presented as that of explaining how the mental can inject causal influences into the causally closed physical domain, that is, the problem of explaining mental-to-physical causation. I wanted to do something more, namely to show that physicalism can put in peril all forms of mental causation, including mental-to-mental causation.[7] This is why the argument begins with line (1). It is at Stage 2 that we take up mental-to-physical causation. It is noteworthy that,

7. As we will see in the next chapter, an interesting parallel holds in the case of substance dualism: under substance dualism, mental-to-mental causation turns out to be as problematic as mental-to-physical causation.

unlike in the second stage below, the argument up to this point makes no explicit appeal to any special metaphysical principles; in particular, no specific assumptions about the physical domain, such as its causal closure or completeness, enter the picture at this stage.[8] Mental-physical supervenience is the only substantive premise that has been in play thus far.

Stage 2

There are two ways of completing the argument, and I believe the second, which is new, is of some interest. I will first present the original version in a somewhat clearer form:

COMPLETION I

We now turn our attention to M, the supposed mental cause of M*. From *Supervenience*, it follows:

(4) M has a physical supervenience base, P.

There are strong reasons for thinking that P is a cause of P*. I will not rehearse the considerations in support of this idea; let us just note that P is (at least) nomologically sufficient for M, and the occurrence of M on this occasion depends on, and is determined by, the presence of P on this occasion. Since ex hypothesi M is a cause of P*, P would appear amply to qualify as a cause of P* as well. So we have:

(5) M causes P*, and P causes P*.

8. On some occasions I have tried to argue for (3) by invoking an exclusion principle—see, for example, the "principle of determinative/generative exclusion" in chapter 1. I think it preferable not to appeal to any general principle here; I now prefer to rely on the reader's seeing the tension I spoke of in connection with the two answers to the question "Why is M* instantiated on this occasion?" Anyone who understands Jonathan Edwards's argument and his mirror analogy will see it; I don't believe invoking any "principle" will help persuade anyone who is not with me here.

Note that P's causation of P* cannot be thought of as a causal chain with M as an intermediate causal link; one reason is that the P-to-M relation is not a causal relation. Note also that since M supervenes on P, M and P occur precisely at the same time. (Moreover, as we will shortly see, the two principles that will be introduced, *Exclusion* and *Closure*, together disqualify M as a cause of P*, making the idea of a causal chain from P to M to P* a nonstarter.)

To continue, from *Irreducibility*, we have:

(6) $M \neq P$.[9]

Again, (5) and (6) present to us a situation with metaphysical tension. For P* is represented here as having two distinct causes, each sufficient for its occurrence. The situation is ripe for the application of the causal exclusion principle, which can be stated as follows:

> *Exclusion*. No single event can have more than one sufficient cause occurring at any given time—unless it is a genuine case of causal overdetermination.

Let us assume that this is not a case of causal overdetermination (we will discuss the overdetermination issue below).

(7) P* is not causally overdetermined by M and P.

By *Exclusion*, therefore, we must eliminate either M or P as P*'s cause. Which one?

---

9. Note: this only means that this instance of $M \neq$ this instance of P. Does this mean that a Davidsonian "token identity" suffices here? The answer is no: the relevant sense in which an instance of $M =$ an instance of P requires either property identity $M = P$ or some form of reductive relationship between them. (See *Mind in a Physical World*, ch. 4). The fact that properties M and P must be implicated in the identity, or nonidentity, of M and P instances can be seen from the fact that "An M-instance causes a P-instance" must be understood with the proviso "in virtue of the former being an instance of M and the latter an instance of P."

(8) The putative mental cause, M, is excluded by the physical cause, P. That is, P, not M, is a cause of P*.

We can give relatively informal reasons for choosing P over M as the cause of P*, but for a general theoretical justification we may appeal to the causal closure of the physical domain:

> *Closure.* If a physical event has a cause that occurs at t, it has a physical cause that occurs at t.[10]

If we were to choose M over P as P*'s cause, *Closure* would kick in again, leading us to posit a physical cause of P*, call it P_1 (what could P_1 be if not P?), and this would again call for the application of *Exclusion*, forcing us to choose between M and P_1 (that is, P). Unless P is chosen and M excluded, we would be off to an unending repetition of the same choice situation; M must be excluded and P retained.

It is worthwhile to reflect on how *Exclusion* and *Closure* work together to yield the epiphenomenalist conclusion (8). *Exclusion* itself is neutral with respect to the mental-physical competition; it says either the mental cause or the physical cause must go, but doesn't favor either over the other. What makes the difference— what introduces an asymmetry into the situation—is *Closure*. It is the causal closure of the physical world that excludes the mental cause, enabling the physical cause to prevail. If the situation with causal closure were the reverse, so that it was the mental domain, not the physical domain, that was causally closed, the mental

---

10. For discussion of physical causal closure, or "completeness," see, e.g., David Papineau, *Thinking about Consciousness* (Oxford: Clarendon Press, 2002), ch. 1; E. J. Lowe, "Physical Causal Closure and the Invisibility of Mental Causation," in *Physicalism and Mental Causation*, ed. Sven Walter and Heinz-Dieter Heckmann (Exeter, UK: Imprint Academic, 2003). A simpler statement of causal closure in the form "If a physical event has a cause, it has a physical cause" will not do; given the transitivity of causation, the requirement would be met by a causal chain consisting of a physical effect caused by a mental cause which in turn is caused by a physical cause.

cause would have prevailed over its physical competitor. I suppose this could happen under some forms of Idealism; one would then worry about the "problem" of physical causation.

COMPLETION 2

Let us begin with the last line of Stage 1:

(3) M causes M* by causing its physical
   supervenience base P*.

From which it follows:

(4) M is a cause of P*.

By *Closure* it follows:

(5) P* has a physical cause—call it P—occurring
   at the time M occurs.

(6) M ≠ P (by *Irreducibility*).

(7) Hence, P* has two distinct causes, M and P,
   and this is not a case of causal overdetermination.

(8) Hence, by *Exclusion*, either M or P must go.

(9) By *Closure* and *Exclusion*, M must go; P stays.

This is simpler than Completion 1. *Supervenience* is not needed as a premise, and the claim that M's supervenience base P has a valid claim to be a cause of P* has been bypassed, making it unnecessary to devise an argument for it. However, Completion 1, in some ways, is more intuitive; it better captures Jonathan Edwards's fundamental insight and makes it particularly salient how putative higher-level causal relations give way to causal processes at a lower level. Either way, the main significance of Stage 2 lies in what it shows about the possible hazards involved in the idea of "downward" causation, namely that *the assumptions of causal exclusion and lower-level causal closure disallow downward causation.*

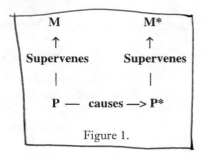

Figure 1.

Figure 1 pictures the outcome of the argument under Completion 1. In this picture, there is but one causal relation, from physical property P to another physical property P*, and the initially posited causal relation from M to M* has been eliminated. An apparent causal relation between the two mental properties is explained away by their respective supervenience on two physical properties that are connected by a genuine causal process. In this picture neither M nor M* is implicated in any causal relations; they play no role in shaping the causal structure—they only supervene on properties that constitute that structure. The supervenience relations together with the causal relation involved can generate counterfactual dependencies between the two mental properties, and between them and the physical properties; but these are no more causal than counterfactual dependencies involving any other supervenient property and its subvenient base (compare the aesthetic properties of a work of art and their base physical properties). Completion 2 presents a picture that is a bit less full: we no longer have the vertical "supervenience" arrow from P to M. M of course must have a physical supervenience base, but the argument, unlike in Completion 1, does not require it to be a cause of P*, although, as Completion 1 suggests, it may well be. The moral, however, is the same: the $M \rightarrow M^*$ and $M \rightarrow P^*$ causal relations have given way to an underlying physical causal process, $P \rightarrow P^*$.

IS OVERDETERMINATION AN OPTION?

Several critics have taken issue with line (7), in both completions of the argument, where the claim is made that we should not think of M and P as two distinct overdetermining causes of P*. One thing I said to defend this claim in *Mind in a Physical World* was this: taking the overdetermination option would be in violation of *Closure*, for in a world in which P does not occur but which is as close to the actual world as possible, M would be a cause of P*, leaving P* without a physical cause. My critics have convinced me that what I said there is not quite right and at best incomplete.

Ned Block asks whether in the supposed possible world, one in which the supervenience base P of M does not occur, M could be thought of as occurring at all. If we take away the supervenience base of M, shouldn't that also take away M? This is something to think about. If what Block has in mind is that the following counterfactual may well be true, I agree:

(C)   If P had not occurred, M would not have occurred.

For we are apt to reason like this: M was there because P was there, so take away P and M goes as well. "If the patient's nociceptive neurons had not been stimulated at *t*, he would not have experienced pain at *t*," uttered, say, when we deliberately activated these neurons in an experimental situation, would evidently be true. In considering the claim that M and P are each a sufficient cause of P*, however, we need to be able to consider a possible situation in which M occurs without P and evaluate the claim that in this possible situation P* nonetheless follows. If such is not a possible situation—that is, if of necessity any nonP-world is ipso facto a nonM-world—what significance can we attach to the claim that P and M are each an overdetermining sufficient cause of P*, that in addition to P, M also is a sufficient cause of P*? *Supervenience* does not render a nonP-world in which M occurs impossible; all that *Supervenience* requires is that such a world must include an alternative physical base of M. So suppose W is a world in which M occurs but P does not. In an instructive and helpful discussion, Thomas Crisp and Ted Warfield have the following to say about such worlds:

> Consider though: either [*Supervenience*] holds in W or it does not. Suppose it does. It follows that M has a physical supervenience base P' in W. What is the causal status of P' vis-à-vis P* in W? We won't repeat ourselves, but we saw above an argument of Kim's to the effect that if P' is a supervenience base for M and M causes P*, then P' is also causally sufficient for P*. If [*Supervenience*] holds in W, therefore, P* does have a physical cause in W, and [*Closure*] therefore does not fail in W.[11]

Crisp and Warfield are right. Notice, though, that in W, we have a replay of exactly the same situation with which we began—M has a physical base, P', threatening to preempt it as a cause of P*. In any world in which *Supervenience* holds and M causes P*, some physical property, instantiated at the same time, can claim to be a sufficient cause of P*. As long as *Supervenience* is held constant, there is no world in which M by itself, independently of a physical base, brings about P*; whenever M claims to be a cause of P*, there is some physical property waiting to claim at least an equal causal status. In the actual world, we may suppose that a continuous causal chain connects P with P* (in some cases we may already have detailed neurophysiological knowledge of the physical causal process leading from P to P*).[12] And it would be incoherent to suppose there is another

11. Thomas M. Crisp and Ted A. Warfield, "Kim's Master Argument," *Noûs* 35 (2001): 304–16 (the quoted passage appears on p. 314).

12. In introducing consideration of causal chains, I am implicitly asking the reader to think of causation in terms of actual productive/generative mechanisms involving energy flow, momentum transfer, and the like, and not merely in terms of counterfactual dependencies. Needless to say, the overdetermination idea makes little sense when causation is understood this way.

causal chain from M to P* that is independent of the causal
process connecting P with P*; the only plausible supposition is
that if there is a causal path from M to P*, that must coincide
with the causal path from P to P*. In W, another causal chain
connects P' with P*, and the M-P* chain must coincide with
that, and similarly in other such worlds. To be a cause of P*, M
must somehow ride piggyback on physical causal chains—
distinct ones depending on which physical property subserves
M on a given occasion, in the same world or in other possible
worlds. And we may ask: In virtue of what relation it bears to
physical property P does M earn its entitlement to a free ride
on the causal chain from P to P* and to claim this causal chain
to be its own? Obviously, the only significant relation M bears
to P is supervenience. But why should supervenience confer
this right on M? The fact of the matter is that there is only one
causal process here, from P to P*,[13] and M's supposed causal
contribution to the production of P* is totally mysterious. In
standard cases of overdetermination, like two bullets hitting the
victim's heart at the same time, the short circuit and the over-
turned lantern causing a house fire, and so on, each overdetermining cause plays a distinct and distinctive causal role. The
usual notion of overdetermination involves two or more separate and independent causal chains intersecting at a common
effect. Because of *Supervenience*, however, that is not the kind
of situation we have here. In this sense, this is not a case of
genuine causal overdetermination, and *Exclusion* applies in a
straightforward way. Moreover, anyone tempted by the idea
that mental events make their causal contributions by being

13. Some have suggested that the M-to-P* causation is a higher-level "redescription" of the causal process from P to P*. E.g., John R. Searle, "Consciousness, the Brain and the Connection Principle: A Reply," *Philosophy and
Phenomenological Research* 55 (1995): 217–32, especially 218–19. Obviously, the
redescription strategy is available only to those who accept "M = P," namely
reductionist physicalists (Searle of course does not count himself among
them).

overdetermining causes should reflect on whether this option could sufficiently vindicate the causal efficacy of the mental.

Now for the second leg of Crisp and Warfield's dilemma:

> Now suppose that [*Supervenience*] does not hold in W. And suppose further that, just as Kim suggests, M causes P* in W without there being any physical cause of P*. Given these assumptions, [*Closure*] does indeed fail in W. But recall that we have supposed along with Kim that the actual world is a Supervenience-world. It follows from this supposition that W is either nomologically or metaphysically impossible, depending on how we read the relevant modal operator in the formulation of [*Supervenience*]. So if W is a world in which [*Closure*] is violated in the way Kim suggests, W is at least nomologically impossible.
>
> What should nonreductivist fans of overdetermination think about this? Should they give up their view because it implies that [*Closure*] fails in worlds that are nomologically (and maybe even metaphysically) impossible? We can't see why they should.[14]

I think we can set aside the possibility that mind-body supervenience is logically or metaphysically necessary, since such a view is essentially a reductionist view,[15] and we are here considering *Supervenience* as a part of nonreductive physicalism. Let us assume then that *Supervenience* is nomologically necessary, and that it fails in W. So in virtue of violating *Supervenience*, W is nomologically impossible. However, W is nomologically impossible not because some physical law is violated in W but because some mental properties fail to supervene on physical properties—that is, because some psychophysical laws of our world fail in W. So W may well be a physically possible world; in fact, we may stipulate W to be a perfect duplicate of our

14. Crisp and Warfield, "Kim's Master Argument," p. 314.

15. This is not an uncontroversial issue, but we cannot go into it here. And there are independent reasons for thinking that mind-brain supervenience, if it holds, must be construed as nomological, not logical or metaphysical, supervenience.

world in all physical respects, including spacetime structure, basic physical laws, and fundamental particles. Should the physicalist not care whether physical causal closure holds in a world like W? Contrary to what Crisp and Warfield suggest, it seems obvious to me that anyone who cares about physicalism should care very much about *Closure* in W.

A more direct way of ruling out overdetermination as an option is to adopt a stronger form of physical causal closure:

> *Strong closure.* Any cause of a physical event is itself a physical event—that is, no nonphysical event can be a cause of a physical event.[16]

Using this principle as a premise has two significant effects. First, it stops the overdetermination option in its tracks; *Strong closure* by itself disallows mental-to-physical causation. Second, *Strong closure* allows us to dispense with *Exclusion*. We no longer need this principle to exclude M in favor of P as P*'s cause, for the simple reason that *Strong closure*, in conjunction with *Irreducibility*, makes M ineligible as a cause of P*.

How might the supervenience argument go under *Strong closure*? Stage 1 is unaffected. Let's briefly look at how Completion 1 might go with *Strong closure*:

(3) M causes M* by causing P*.

(4) M has a physical supervenience base, P.

(5) M causes P*, and P causes P*.

Up to here, the argument is the same as before; from here the argument can continue as follows:

(6*) For every physical property P, M ≠ P *Irreducibility*.

(7*) M does not cause P* (from (6*) and *Strong closure*).

16. An even stronger form of closure can be obtained by also prohibiting physical events from having mental effects—that is, by disallowing all "mixed" causal chains, chains with both physical and mental events.

(8*) M does not cause M* (from (3)[17] and (7*)).

(9*) P causes P* (from (5)).

The outcome is the same as in the original Completion 1, namely Figure 1. But the argument has been simplified in that *Exclusion* has been dispensed with as a premise.

Is this a reason to prefer *Strong closure* to *Closure*? The answer, I believe, is yes and no. Although the causal exclusion principle has been widely accepted and I believe it is virtually an analytic truth with not much content, some find it problematic, and the fact that *Strong closure* makes *Exclusion* dispensable is a point in its favor. (This need not be taken to mean that the argument is no longer properly called an "exclusion" argument; even though no exclusion principle is used as a premise, the *outcome* of the argument is that mental causal relations are "excluded" by physical causality.) Further, there seems no reason for the physicalist to object to *Strong closure*; so why not trade the two premises, *Closure* and *Exclusion*, for a single premise, *Strong closure*, and in the process defuse the overdetermination issue? I believe, though, that there is a philosophical gain in staying with the weaker closure premise. Adopting *Strong closure* as a premise is like starting your argument with mind-body causation already ruled out, at least for nonreductivists; with *Strong closure* as your starting point, there isn't very much more distance you can go or need to go. Perhaps philosophical arguments never make converts out of those who are already committed to the opposite side; but I believe that it can serve philosophical interest to begin with a set of premises that are individually as weak as possible but which somehow conspire together to yield the desired conclusion. It is better, that is to say, to distribute the burden of defending a conclusion among a set of relatively weak premises than to place it on fewer but individually stronger premises.

17. It is implicit in (3) that this is the *only* way M can cause M*.

The latter strategy is apt to provoke the complaint that the argument begs the question and that it serves no useful purpose. I think we learn something about the issues and desiderata involved and their interplay when we run the supervenience argument with *Closure* rather than *Strong closure*.

THE GENERALIZATION ARGUMENT

My main aim in this chapter is to respond to the argument Block has put forward in the following passage:

> The Exclusion Principle [the thesis that "sufficient causation at one level excludes sufficient causation at another level"] leads to problems about causal powers draining away. Kim discusses a number of such problems, including the following two. First, it is hard to believe that there is no mental causation, no physiological causation, no molecular causation, no atomic causation but only bottom level physical causation. Second, it is hard to believe that there is no causation at all if there is no bottom level of physics.[18]

Why does Block think that if the supervenience argument holds, there will be no physiological causation, no molecular causation, etc. any more than mental causation? Because he subscribes to what is called the "generalization argument"—the idea that the supervenience argument generalizes beyond mind-body causation, with the result that causation at *any* level gives way to causation at the next lower level (if there is one), just as the supposed causation at the mental level gets eliminated in favor of causation at the physical/biological level. Block is not alone here. A number of writers have expressed the view that if the supposed problem of mental causation is a real problem, a parallel problem should arise for all other special

18. Block, "Do Causal Powers Drain Away?" p. 138.

sciences, except causation at the most fundamental physical level.[19] Such a view is often stated against the backdrop of a "layered" model of the domains of science, according to which objects and properties of the world are arrayed in a hierarchy of "levels," with the basic physical particles and their properties at the bottom level and, above it, the levels of atoms, molecules, cells, organisms, and so on, all ordered in an ascending ladder-like structure. It is this hierarchical view of the domains of science that gives meaning to the talk of "higher" and "lower" levels—in regard to sciences, laws, explanations, and the rest.[20]

On a hierarchical picture of levels like this, it is natural to think of mental causation only as a special case of higher-level causation. If the supervenience argument shows causation at the psychological level to be preempted by causation at the biological level, why couldn't the argument be iterated to show biological causation to be preempted by physicochemical causation, and so on down to the fundamental microphysical level? The idea that the argument is generalizable this way gains force from the widely accepted assumption that properties at upper levels are supervenient on lower-level properties, the eponymous premise that plays a crucial role in the argument.

Let me begin my response by pointing out that if indeed the supervenience argument is generalizable, that only shows that

19. This includes Tyler Burge, Robert Van Gulick, and many others. See my *Mind in a Physical World*, ch. 3 for references and discussion. Among other discussions of the generalization argument are Paul Noordhof, "Micro-Based Properties and the Supervenience Argument," *Proceedings of the Aristotelian Society* 99 (1999): 109–114; Carl Gillett, "Does the Argument from Realization Generalize? Responses to Kim," *Southern Journal of Philosophy* 39 (2001): 79–98; Thomas D. Bontly, "The Supervenience Argument Generalizes," *Philosophical Studies* 109 (2002): 75–96.

20. Whether a layered model of this kind can be developed as a comprehensive ontology of the world is a debatable issue. I discuss some of the difficulties with such an approach in "The Layered Model: Metaphysical Considerations," *Philosophical Explorations* 5 (2002): 2–20. See also John Heil, *From an Ontological Point of View* (Oxford: Oxford University Press, 2003), ch. 4.

we have a general philosophical problem on hand, and that it is not necessarily a refutation of the argument. If the argument goes wrong, one would like to know just where and how it goes wrong. Moreover, just saying that there "obviously" are biological causation, physiological causation, and so on isn't very helpful; what has to be shown is that these kinds of "higher-level" causation are irreducible to basic physical causation—namely, that there are these causal relations *in addition to* the underlying physical causal processes. It is important to keep in mind that the supervenience argument assumes among its premises the doctrine of the irreducibility of the mental; this premise is invoked at line (6) in both completions of Stage 2. As may be recalled, the argument begins with the supposition that an instance of a mental property M causes another mental property M* to instantiate (line (1)). Block says that this M-to-M* causal relation is "putative—it is a premise in a *reductio* that Kim will reject."[21] But this is not the full story: there is another premise, the premise of irreducibility (line (6): $M \neq P$), against which a reductio can also be performed. This premise, not the supposed M-to-M* causal relation, has always been my primary target. The real aim of the argument, as far as my own philosophical interests are concerned, is not to show that mentality is epiphenomenal, or that mental causal relations are eliminated by physical causal relations; it is rather to show "either reduction or causal impotence." To put it another way, my aim is to force a choice between the situation depicted in figure 1 and what is pictured in figure 2. In this picture, the $M \rightarrow M*$ causation remains genuine and real; it is the very same causal relation as $P \rightarrow P*$; the reduction collapses the two levels into one, and there is here one causal relation, not two. The aim of the supervenience argument is to clarify the options available to the physicalist: If you deem yourself a

21. Block, "Do Causal Powers Drain Away?" p. 134.

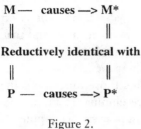

Figure 2.

physicalist, you must choose between figure 1 and figure 2. There are no other options.[22]

Indeed, the supervenience argument may be generalizable, but all that would show is that if there is biological causation, biological properties are, or are reducible to, physical or physicochemical properties; it does not show that biological causation does not exist. The epiphenomenalist brunt of the argument is avoided if one is prepared, and is able, to choose the reductionist branch of the dilemma. It should be kept in mind that merely "choosing" reductionism doesn't make reductionism true; whether or not reductionism is sustainable as an option is an independent question that ought to be decided on its merits.

Many philosophers will reply that biological properties are no more physically reducible than psychological properties, citing their "multiple realizability" in relation to physicochemical properties. For most antireductionist philosophers, multiple realizability has long been a mantra, an all-purpose antireductionist argument applied across the board to all special science properties. They see multiple realization everywhere, and this

22. The underlying metaphysical moral of the two options is the same, however: there is only one causal relation here, namely a physical one, and, more generally, causality is fundamentally a physical phenomenon. An interestingly similar picture results from Donald Davidson's thesis that causation requires "strict laws," and that strict laws are found only in physics. See his "Mental Events," in *Essays on Actions and Events* (Oxford and New York: Oxford University Press, 1980).

leads them to see irreducibility everywhere. I believe, however, that the notion of "realization" as it is often invoked in this context is too loose and ill-formed, and that when realization is properly understood, multiple realization only leads to reducibility to multiple reduction bases, not to irreducibility.[23]

Considerations like those motivating the supervenience argument do not have eliminative implications for macrocausation in general; the supervenience argument does not eliminate all macrocausation, leaving only causal relations between microentities and their properties. This baseball has causal powers that none of its proper parts, in particular none of its constituent microparticles, have, and in virtue of its mass and hardness, the baseball can break a window when it strikes it with a certain velocity. The shattering of the glass was caused by the baseball and certainly not by the individual particles composing it. True, the baseball is a composite object made up of its constituent molecules, atoms, particles, or what have you, and this complex structure consisting of microparticles broke the window. But there is no mystery here: the baseball = this composite structure of microparticles.[24] Presumably, the causal powers of the baseball are *determined* by its microstructural features and perhaps also *explainable* in terms of them. But determination or explanation need have no eliminative implications. Perhaps, macrocausal relations are constituted by, or composed of, a bunch of microcausal relations. But that does not banish macrocausation out of existence any more than the fact that the baseball is composed of microparticles entails its nonexistence. All this is consistent with the supervenience argument.

23. See my "Multiple Realization and the Metaphysics of Reduction," *Philosophy and Phenomenological Research* 52 (1992): 1–26, and *Mind in a Physical World*, ch. 4. For further discussion of multiple realizability and reduction, see John Bickle, *Psychoneural Reduction: The New Wave* (Cambridge, MA: MIT Press, 1998).

24. For a dissenting view—*plus* the view that macrocausation is in general preempted by microcausation—see Trenton Merricks, *Objects and Persons* (Oxford: Clarendon, 2001).

BLOCK'S CAUSAL DRAINAGE ARGUMENT

A micro-based property of an object is a property characterizing its microstructure—it tells us what sorts of microconstituents the object is made up of and the structural relations that configure these constituents into a stable object with substantival unity. Micro-based (or microstructural) properties of an object are its macroproperties—they belong to the whole object, not to its constituents—and, moreover, they do not supervene on the properties of the object's micro-constituents. For that reason, the supervenience argument does not touch micro-based properties,[25] and I have claimed that this prevents causal powers from seeping downward from level to level, from macro to micro. Further, I have argued that many chemical and biological properties seem construable as micro-based properties, properties defined or analyzable in terms of microstructure. Block recognizes this as my strategy. The initial criticism he advances can be called the "multiple composition" argument. He writes:

> But why can't micro-based properties be micro-based in *alternative ways*? Why isn't jade an example of a micro-based property, micro-based in both calcium magnesium silicate (nephrite) and sodium aluminum silicate (jadeite)?. . .
>
> My doubts about [Kim's] picture center on the worry just mentioned concerning multiple decomposition. Micro-based properties are supposed to prevent draining away for both supervenient and functional properties, but Kim's plugging the draining with micro-based properties depends on assuming identities (such as "water = H_2O") and multiple composition will preclude such identities.[26]

---

25. This has been disputed by some of the authors cited in footnote 19.
26. Block, "Do Causal Powers Drain Away?" pp. 145–46.

Here Block appears to be thinking of multiple composition in parallel with multiple realization: just as multiple realization has been used as an argument against reducibility, multiple composition could be used against identifying a macroproperty, say being jade, with micro-based properties. This is an interesting possibility; multiple compositionality may work as well as multiple realizability, each against its reductionist target. However, I think that neither works very well.

There are two things to say about Block's argument. First, in spite of jade's multiple composition, each instance of jade—that is, each individual piece of jade—is either jadeite or nephrite, and I don't see anything wrong about identifying *its* being jade with *its* being nephrite (if it is nephrite) or with *its* being jadeite (if it's jadeite). If it is nephrite, the causal powers that it has in virtue of being jade will be exactly identical with the causal powers of nephrite. All we need is identity at the level of instances, not necessarily at the level of kinds and properties; causation after all is a relation between property or kind-instances, not between properties or kinds as such. Second, suppose a macroproperty has two or more distinct micro-compositions. We can use the jade example again: we presumably distinguish between the two compositions, jadeite and nephrite, importantly because they are *causally* distinguishable— that is, jadeite and nephrite have significantly different causal profiles. Given this, there are two options. We can either deny that jade is a genuine kind (at least, jade is not a kind of mineral), on account of its causal heterogeneity, or identify jade with a disjunctive kind, jadeite or nephrite (that is, being jade is identified with having the microstructure of jadeite or the microstructure of nephrite). The second option which allows disjunctive kinds is a more conservative approach and may be more viable as a general solution. On the disjunctive approach, being jade turns out to be a causally heterogeneous property, not a causally inert one, and jade turns out to be a causally heterogeneous kind, not a causally irrelevant one. To disarm

Block's multiple composition argument, adopting either disjunctive property/kind identities or instance (or token) identities seems sufficient.

This, however, does not fully block the drainage argument. There may be no causal seepage from macro to micro, but that is not the only way the seepage can occur. The trouble can be seen when we recognize that a given object can have micro-based properties at various levels (the biological, the physicochemical, the atomic, etc.), and that higher-level micro-based properties arguably supervene on their lower-level counterparts. Block has this in mind, I think, when he speaks of "endless subvenience."[27] Other commentators, in particular Ausonio Marras,[28] have also made this point. Let us see how the idea might be developed.

Take any macro-object, O, and let a *total* micro-based property *at level L* be the property corresponding to a complete description of O's microstructure at level L. (Roughly, we can think of "levels" in terms of modes of decomposition of material objects into physically significant constituents; examples of levels are the molecular level, the atomic level, and the level of basic particles.) So if L is the level of the Standard Model, a total micro-based property of O at this level would give a complete description of O's microstructure in terms of the particles and forces posited in the Standard Model. The following is a plausible physicalist principle:

> *Macro-micro supervenience.* All intrinsic properties of O, at any level higher than L, supervene on the total micro-based property of O at level L.

The idea is that wholes made up of the same (qualitatively identical) constituents configured in the same structural relationships

27. Block, "Do Causal Powers Drain Away?" p. 140.
28. Ausonio Marras in "Critical Notice of *Mind in a Physical World*," *Canadian Journal of Philosophy* 30 (2000): 137–60; see p. 151.

will exhibit an identical set of intrinsic properties. Since micro-based properties are intrinsic properties, it follows:

> For any object O, O's micro-based properties at level L supervene on O's total micro-based property at level L^*, where $L^* < L$.

Consider a series of total micro-based properties of a given object: M_L, M_{L-1}, M_{L-2}, ... Suppose this series has no end; it continues on, without ever reaching a bottom level. That is, let us suppose that the speculation of the physicists cited by Block is correct, and that matter is infinitely divisible (I will go along with Block that all this makes perfectly good sense; but can we really make sense of the idea of an object that is literally made up of infinitely many physically significant parts, here and now?) According to the supervenience argument, M_L apparently cedes its causal powers to M_{L-1}, whose causal powers in turn are taken over by those of M_{L-2}, and so on without end.

Here, Block's worry appears well placed. The supervenience argument implies the following general proposition:

> *Seepage.* If property Q supervenes on a property Q^* at a lower level without being reducible to it, Q's causal powers are preempted by those of Q^*.

This means that no member of the infinite series of total micro-based properties M_L, M_{L-1}, ... has causal powers, since every member has a lower member on which it supervenes. If no member of this series has causal powers, there are none to be had anywhere in the series. Moreover, since all intrinsic properties of the object in question are assumed to supervene on its total micro-based properties at lower levels, none of the object's intrinsic properties can have causal powers, and that means that the object itself has no causal powers. All this on the premise that microphysics has no bottom level and matter is infinitely divisible.[29]

---

29. For an interesting (skeptical) discussion of the existence of a bottom level, see Jonathan Schaffer, "Is There a Fundamental Level?" *Noûs* 37 (2003): 498–517.

This, I believe, is Block's argument, or at least it is a close-enough approximation to it. As Marras has pointed out, it seems possible to develop the generalization argument within a single level in the micro-macro hierarchy. In any case, the argument is worth thinking about. Compare *Seepage* with the following alternative ways of conceiving the interlevel causal relationship:

> *Explanation.* If property Q supervenes on a property Q* at a lower level without being reducible to it, Q's causal powers (and the causal relations into which Q enters) can be *explained* in terms of the causal powers of Q*.

> *Constitution.* If Q supervenes on Q*, Q's causal powers are *constituted* by those of Q*.

> *Derivation/determination.* If Q supervenes on Q*, Q's causal powers *derive from*, and are *determined by* and *dependent on*, those of Q*.

It is interesting to note that, unlike *Seepage*, none of these alternatives seem to be vulnerable to the drainage argument. The reason is that these alternatives, insofar as we understand them, don't appear to have eliminative implications for causation at the higher, supervenient levels. For example, the fact that Q's causal powers are "explained" by the causal powers of its underlying base Q* does not mean that the former are in any sense preempted or eliminated by the latter, or even that they are somehow reduced to the latter. Exactly what "constitution"[30] might mean, or what "derivation" and "dependence" amount to, requires further thought, but it is clear that these

---

30. For a defense of nonreductive physicalism based on the idea of constitution, see Derk Pereboom, "Robust Nonreductive Physicalism," *Journal of Philosophy* 99 (2002): 499–531. I believe that the main burden, which is yet to be discharged, of this approach is to produce a serviceably clear concept of constitution. See also Lynne Rudder Baker, *Persons and Bodies: A Constitution View* (Cambridge: Cambridge University Press, 2000).

terms as understood in their rough ordinary philosophical senses have no obviously eliminative intimations.

So why not embrace one or another, or perhaps a combination, of these alternative ways of conceiving the interlevel causal relationships? That would stop the drainage right at the start, and whether there is, or is not, a bottom level makes no difference. So why not say that M, though it doesn't quite have the causal status of P in relation to P*, is a "derivative" cause of P* in virtue of its supervenience on P? M is not in itself an independent cause of P*; its causal status derives from its supervenience on the causally active P. Some years back, I thought that this might be a plausible way of vindicating mental causation.[31] This was the model of so-called supervenient causation. But it soon began to dawn on me that this was an empty verbal ploy; we can "say," if we want, that M is a "supervenient" cause, "dependent" or "derivative" cause, or whatever, and we can embellish *figure 1* by drawing a horizontal arrow connecting M with M*, with the annotation "superveniently causes," as in figure 3. But this is only a gimmick with no meaning; the facts are as represented in the unadorned figure 1, and inserting a dotted arrow and calling it "supervenient" causation, or anything else (how about "pretend" or "faux" causation), does not alter the situation one bit. It neither adds any new facts nor reveals any hitherto unnoticed relationships. Inserting the extra arrow is not only pointless; it could also be philosophically pernicious if it should mislead us into thinking that we have thereby conferred on M, the mental event, some real causal role. Moreover, embracing this approach would lead us back to the over-determination/exclusion problem—unless we simply stipulate the problem away by declaring that supervenient causal relations do not compete with the causal relation underlying them.

31. In, e.g., "Epiphenomenal and Supervenient Causation," *Midwest Studies in Philosophy* 9 (1984): 257–270. See also Ernest Sosa, "Mind-Body Interaction and Supervenient Causation," *Midwest Studies in Philosophy* 9 (1984): 271–81.

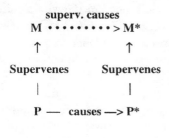

Figure 3.

Jonathan Edwards would have approved my position: in his argument against persisting objects, he did not settle for derivative or dependent causation between created substances; he felt, rightly, that God wholly preempted causation at "higher" levels. What is Block's own position in regard to these issues? He writes:

> But there is another point of view that recognizes causal efficacy at many levels and does not regard them as competing. And this latter point of view also avoids the problem of causal powers draining away.[32]

And, concerning the "tension" I described at steps (1) and (2) of the supervenience argument, Block writes: "Of course, the non-reductive materialist who accepts causation at many levels should not recognize any tension."[33]

Block's position is the favored approach of most nonreductive physicalists; however, this popular position is precisely what is being challenged. The nonreductive physicalist who accepts supervenience *ought to* recognize the tension; in view of

---

32. Block, "Do Causal Powers Drain Away?" p. 149. Terence Horgan, among others, holds a similar view; see his "Nonreductive Physicalism and the Explanatory Autonomy of Psychology," in *Naturalism: A Critical Appraisal*, ed. Stephen J. Wagner and Richard Warner (Notre Dame: IN: Notre Dame University Press, 1993).
33. Block, "Do Causal Powers Drain Away?" p. 135.

the considerations advanced in the supervenience argument—
basically, Jonathan Edwards's insight—I believe the nonreductive physicalist owes us an explanation of why there is no tension
here. It would be nice if we could embrace causation at many
levels, including the psychological, the biological, and so on,
and also cross-level causation, both downward and upward, all
of them coexisting in harmony. And it *is* important to us to be
able to have trust in the causal efficacy of our beliefs and desires, emotions and consciousness, and to believe in our powers
as agents in the world—all this without reducing mentality to
mere patterns of electrical activity in the brain. But these are
only a wish list—the starting point of the mental causation debate. The main purpose of the supervenience argument is to
bring into focus the disquieting fact that there are strong metaphysical pressures on our pre-philosophical assumptions and
desiderata in this area. If the argument is correct, it shows that
there are inevitable causal entanglements between different
levels, raising all sorts of issues concerning causal closure, competition, and exclusion, and forcing some significant philosophical choices. The nonreductive materialist must sort out and
come to terms with these issues; ignoring them is not an option
for him. With his drainage argument, Block attempts to defeat
the supervenience argument. That is a first step. But this argument has the form of a reductio: if it works, we will know the
argument cannot be sound, but that will not tell us just where
the argument goes wrong. And this knowledge is required if we
are to construct a positive account of multilevel causation of
the sort that Block and others have in mind.

In any case, what can be said to counter the drainage argument as lately formulated? As far as the dialectics of the mental
causation debate goes, my response here is the same as my
reply to Block's statement that the supervenience argument is a
reductio against its first premise ("Mental property M causes
mental property M*"). As may be recalled, I pointed out
that there is another premise against which a reductio can be

performed, namely the premise of psychophysical irreducibility, and that this was my real target. If, as Block's argument suggests, the supervenience argument can be continued to yield as a further conclusion the following proposition:

(H)   If there is no bottom level in microphysics, there is no causation anywhere.

and if we find (H) unacceptable, that only means that we need to consider which of the premises of the argument is to be rejected. My suggestion again is that the irreducibility premise should be the prime candidate for rejection; I will elaborate on this below.

Before we go on, there is one point that needs to be clarified. Contrary to what seems sometimes assumed, it is not the case that according to my argument, causation at any level L gives way to causation at level $L - 1$ (the next lower level), like the rungs of a ladder that keep collapsing each on top of the next lower one. That this is not the case is seen from the fact that the argument requires *Closure* as a premise—the assumption that the lower level in play is causally closed. This means that the mental rung will not collapse onto the biological rung, as far as the supervenience argument is concerned, for the simple reason that the biological level is not causally closed. The same is true of macrolevel physics and chemistry. It is only when we reach the fundamental level of microphysics that we are likely to get a causally closed domain.[34] As I understand it,

34. Actually various complications arise with the talk of levels in this context. In the only levels scheme that has been worked out with some precision, the hierarchical scheme of Paul Oppenheim and Hilary Putnam (in their "Unity of Science as a Working Hypothesis," *Minnesota Studies in the Philosophy of Science*, vol. 2, Minneapolis: University of Minnesota Press, 1958), it is required that each level includes all mereological aggregates of entities at that level (that is, each level is closed under mereological summation). Thus, the bottom level of elementary particles, in this scheme, is in effect the universal domain that includes molecules, organisms, and the rest.

the so-called Standard Model is currently taken to represent
the bottom level. Assume that this level is causally closed; the
supervenience argument, if it works, shows that mental causal
relations give way to causal relations at this microlevel. And
similarly for biological causation, chemical causation, geologi-
cal causation, and the rest. So as far as the supervenience
argument goes, the bottom level of fundamental particles (assuming that this is the only level that is causally closed) is always the reference physical domain; there is no step-by-step
devolution of causal relations from level to level (I am not suggesting that Block thinks that).[35]

Block's drainage argument evokes some deep metaphysical
associations, and this is part of what makes it so interesting.
Just think of the whole group of celebrated philosophical arguments with a similar structure, going back to Aristotle and
Aquinas. I have in mind Aristotle's argument for the existence
of a "prime mover"—the unmoved mover that is the source of
all motion. If something moves, it is moved by another thing
that moves, which in turn is moved by yet another mover, and
so on; but this series cannot go on ad infinitum, for that would
make motion impossible. So there must be a mover that is itself not moved by anything else. Aquinas's cosmological argument for the existence of God appears to work in a similar
way: there must be a first cause that is itself uncaused because
the causal series cannot extend into the past without end. If it
did, nothing would exist. The classic foundationalist argument, such as we find in Chisholm,[36] for the existence of "basic"
knowledge runs the same way, as do the familiar arguments for

35. A similar problem may well arise for mind-body supervenience; it is
likely that mental properties do not supervene on biological properties alone,
and that to get full supervenience we have to reach further down and include
nonbiological physicochemical properties in the base.

36. Roderick M. Chisholm, *Theory of Knowledge*, 2nd edition (Englewood
Cliffs, NJ: Prentice-Hall, 1977).

the existence of semantic primitives, the existence of intrinsic goods, and the like. I think it would be interesting to analyze the metaphysics and logic of arguments that share this general structure. Here, however, I will only make a couple of points specifically in regard to Block's drainage argument.

The first point concerns causal closure. As earlier noted, a causal collapse to the level below would occur only if the lower level is causally closed. Are we assuming that if matter is infinitely divisible, physics will be causally closed at each level of decomposition? I believe that the physicist David Bohm made the observation that each time we descend to a lower microlevel, we do so because the current level is not causally closed ("explanatorily complete" may be a better term in this context); that is, because there are phenomena at this level that can only be explained by descending to a lower level. If something like that is true, no level in Block's infinitely descending series of levels will be causally closed, or explanatorily complete, and the supervenience argument cannot get a toehold. We would not have the required closure premise available— unless we take as our lowest level the *union* of all the microlevels in this infinite chain. Will such a union be causally closed? It has to be, and I believe it may well give us the bottom level which will stop Block's infinite causal drainage.

Second, we must return to reduction again. For Block's drainage argument to work in full force, it must be assumed that the irreducibility premise will hold for purely physical levels—we must assume that molecular facts are not reducible to atomic facts, that atomic facts are not reducible to facts at the level of the Standard Model, and so on down the line. How plausible is this assumption? There are well-known, though by no means undisputed, arguments for regarding the mental to be physically irreducible, and arguments have been advanced to show that the biological level is irreducible to the physicochemical level. But I know of no argument, other than Block's multiple-composition argument discussed above, to show that the irreducibility assumption will stand as we go down from one microphysical level to the next. The standard view, as I understand it, is that chemistry and macrophysics are reducible, and in fact have already been substantially reduced, to particle physics via quantum mechanics.[37] Unless we have reason to think that irreducibility will hold "all the way down," we have no reason to think that the causal drainage will go on forever. Reduction is the stopper that will plug the cosmic hole through which causal powers might drain away.

In fact, there appear to be presumptive reasons for thinking that reducibility will hold for the kind of infinite series Block has in mind. Let us begin by noting that in various philosophical contexts the identity "the property of being water = the property of being H_2O" is often affirmed and accepted. This identity is accepted presumably on the basis of the fact that water = H_2O. Let us think a bit about what is involved. The property of being H_2O is a total micro-based property of water at the atomic/molecular level; it is the property of being made up of two hydrogen atoms and one oxygen atom in a certain relational structure. Being water is having this kind of microstructure. Having this microstructure is the microstructural essence of water, and being water just is having that structure. We must expect this line of thought to generalize downward, and the following may be one way to flesh it out. Let us say that the property of being H_2O is the total micro-based property of water at the atomic level L (so having M_L = being H_2O). So we have:

(1) Being water = having M_L.

At the next level down, $L-1$, say the level of the Standard Model, hydrogen atoms have a certain microstructural composition as do oxygen atoms, and water has a certain microstructural composition at this level; call it M_{L-1}. Then by the same reasoning that led us to (1), we have:

(2) Being water = having M_{L-1}.

At the level $L-2$, the one below the Standard Model (if there is such a level), water is again going to have a certain microstructure at that level; this is M_{L-2}. We then have:

(3) Being water = having M_{L-2}.

and so on down the line, to M_{L-3} and the rest. These identities in turn imply the following series of identities:

$$M_L = M_{L-1} = M_{L-2} = M_{L-3} \dots .$$

Voilà! These are the identities we need to stop the drainage.

The foregoing is somewhat sketchy and perhaps too quick, and I do not wish to rest my reply to Block's drainage challenge wholly on these rather speculative thoughts. The primary response to the drainage argument is the point that for downward causal drainage to occur, the reduction option must be ruled out for purely physical levels, including microphysical levels, and it is far from obvious that this can be done. In fact, the drainage problem provides us with one more reason to perform a reductio against the irreducibility premise of the supervenience/exclusion argument.

3

The Rejection of Immaterial Minds

A CAUSAL ARGUMENT

THE DEEP DIFFICULTIES that beset contemporary nonreductive physicalism might prompt some of us to explore nonphysicalist alternatives; in fact, the nonreductivist's predicament seems to have injected new vigor into the dualist projects of philosophers with antecedent antiphysicalist sympathies.[1] For the upshot of our considerations on mental causation was that, for the physicalist, there are only two options left: reductionism and epiphenomenalism. With good reason, most philosophers have found neither choice palatable. On one hand, epiphenomenalism strikes most of us as obviously wrong, if not incoherent; the idea that our thoughts, wants, and intentions might lack causal efficacy of any kind is deeply troubling, going as it does against everything we believe about ourselves as agents and cognizers. It is the kind of doctrine—perhaps radical skepticism is another example—that, even if we had to acknowledge it as true, could not serve as a guide to life; it cannot serve as a premise in our practical reasoning, and it is not possible for us

---

1. For example, William Hasker, *The Emergent Self* (Ithaca, NY: Cornell University Press, 1999); Timothy O'Connor, *Persons and Causes* (Oxford and New York: Oxford University Press, 2001).

to live as though it is true.[2] Reductionism, on the other hand, has seemed to many people not much better: if minds turn out to be mere configurations of neurons, silicon chips, or whatever and consciousness and thoughts are simply patterns of electrical activity in some groups of neurons, that doesn't seem much like saving minds as something distinctive, something we value, something that makes us the feeling, thinking, and rule-following creatures that we are. So why not look outside physicalism? But what options are there if we set aside the physicalist picture? Leaving physicalism behind is to abandon ontological physicalism, the view that bits of matter and their aggregates in space-time exhaust the contents of the world. This means that one would be embracing an ontology that posits entities other than material substances—that is, immaterial minds, or souls, outside physical space, with immaterial, nonphysical properties.[3]

Will a dualist ontology of immaterial minds help us with mental causation and consciousness? That is the question I want to consider here. I will argue that ontological dualism provides us with no help at all, and that in fact it makes things worse. My target will be the interactionist dualism of Descartes. I will be focusing on how mental causation fares within the Cartesian scheme. My conclusion will be: Very badly. As for consciousness, my view is that dualist ontologies offer us no special help; they will only prompt us to reformulate the problem, or perhaps lull us into ignoring it. Brief reflection should convince us that the introduction of immaterial souls as bearers of consciousness will not help to mitigate

2. As things turn out, I will be arguing, in the final chapter, that we have to live with a residual form of epiphenomenalism.

3. Here we will not consider neutral monism and other theories that posit a reality that is neither physical nor mental but of which the physical and the mental are two "aspects" or "manifestations." I believe such theories, in addition to introducing something wholly mysterious and ad hoc, do no better than property dualism, and that in fact for our purposes they will likely turn out to be only variants of property dualism.

William James's sense of perplexity about consciousness,[4] or relieve the emergentists' bafflement over the emergence of consciousness. I will not, however, take up the issue of consciousness in regard to immaterial minds; the difficulties that ontological dualism faces with the problem of causality undermine it so seriously, in my view, as to render the question what further work immaterial souls might do entirely moot.

CARTESIAN DUALISM AND MENTAL CAUSATION

We commonly think that we, as persons, have both a mental and a bodily dimension—or mental aspects and material aspects. Something like this dualism of personhood, I believe, is common lore shared across most cultures and religious traditions, although it is seldom articulated in the form of an explicit set of doctrines as in modern western philosophy and some developed theologies. It is often part of this "folk dualism" that we are able to survive bodily deaths, as souls or spirits, and retain all or most of the mental aspects of ourselves, such as memory, the capacity for thought and volition, and traits of character and personality, long after our bodies have crumbled to dust.

Spirits and souls as conceived in popular lore seem not to be entirely without physical properties, if only vestigially physical ones, and are not what Descartes and other philosophical dualists would call souls or minds—wholly immaterial and nonphysical substances with no physical properties whatever. For example, souls are commonly said to *leave* the body when a person dies and *rise upward* toward heaven, indicating that they are thought to have, and be able to change, locations in physical space. And they can be heard and seen, we are told, by people endowed with special powers and in an especially propitious

4. See chapter 1.

frame of mind. Souls are sometimes pictured as balls of bright light, causing the air to stir as they glide through space and even emitting faint unearthly sounds. But souls and spirits depicted in stories and literature, and in films, are not the immaterial minds of the serious dualist. These latter souls are wholly immaterial and entirely outside physical space.

But can we make sense of the idea that an immaterial soul can be in causal commerce with a material body, and that my immaterial mind can causally influence the physicochemical processes going on in my material brain? Doubts about such a possibility are as old as Descartes's interactionist dualism itself. Conventional wisdom in philosophy of mind has it that its inability to account for mental causation was the downfall of Descartes's mind-body dualism. As has often been noted, his radical dualism of mental and material substances was thought to preclude the possibility of causal transaction between them. Princess Elisabeth of Bohemia achieved philosophical immortality by confronting Descartes with her celebrated challenge to explain "how the mind of a man can determine the bodily spirits [i.e., the fluids in the nerves, muscles, etc.] in producing voluntary actions, being only a thinking substance."[5] According to one commentator, Richard A. Watson, the perceived inconsistency of mind-body causation with the radical duality of minds and bodies was not only a major theoretical flaw in Cartesianism but also the historical cause of its decline.[6]

The reason standardly offered for the supposed incoherence of Cartesian interactionist dualism is that it is difficult to

5. Elisabeth to Descartes, 16 May 1643. This quotation is taken from Daniel Garber, "Understanding Interaction: What Descartes Should Have Told Elisabeth," in *Descartes Embodied* (Cambridge: Cambridge University Press, 2001), p. 172. There is an affecting chapter on Princess Elisabeth in Richard Watson's biography of Descartes, *Cogito, Ergo Sum: The Life of René Descartes* (Boston: David R. Godine, 2002).

6. Richard A. Watson, *The Downfall of Cartesianism 1673–1712* (The Hague, Holland: Martinus Nijhoff, 1966).

"conceive" how two substances with such radically diverse natures, one in spacetime with mass, inertia, and the like and the other lacking wholly in material properties and not even in physical space, could exercise causal influence on each other. Apparently, various principles about causation, such as that cause and effect must show a certain degree of mutual affinity or "essential likeness," that there can be no "greater reality" in an effect than there is in its cause, or that physical causation requires the impact of one body upon another, seem to have played a role. Anthony Kenny, a philosopher well known for his philosophical acuity as well as historical erudition, writes:

> On Descartes' principles it is difficult to see how an unextended thinking substance can cause motion in an extended unthinking substance and how the extended unthinking substance can cause sensations in the unextended thinking substance. The properties of the two kinds of substance seem to place them in such diverse categories that it is impossible for them to interact.[7]

The trouble is that this is all that Kenny has to say about Descartes's difficulties with mind-body causation—and, as far as I know, that is pretty much all we get from Descartes's critics and commentators. But as an argument this is incomplete and unsatisfying. As it stands, it is not much of an argument; rather, it only expresses a vague, inchoate dissatisfaction of the sort that ought to prompt us to look for a real argument. Why is it incoherent to think that there can be causal interaction between things in "diverse categories"? Why is it "impossible" for things with diverse natures to enter into causal relations with one another? What sorts or degrees of diverseness make trouble and why?

It has not been an easy matter to pin down exactly what is wrong with positing causal relations between substances with unlike natures, and explain in concrete terms what it is about

7. Anthony Kenny, *Descartes* (New York: Random House, 1968), pp. 222–23.

the natures of mental and material substance that make them unfit to enter into causal relations with each other. And there have been commentators who have defended Descartes against charges of incoherence like Kenny's. Louis Loeb is one of them.[8] Loeb's defense rests on his claim that Descartes was a proto-Humean about causation—namely that, for Descartes, causality amounted to nothing more than brute regularity, or "constant conjunction," and there can be no a priori metaphysical constraints, such as resemblance or mutual affinity, on what events can be causally joined with what other events. Loeb supports his interpretation with this passage from Descartes:

> There is no reason to be surprised that certain motions of the heart should be naturally connected in this way with certain thoughts, which they in no way resemble. The soul's natural capacity for union with a body brings with it the possibility of an association between thoughts and bodily motions or conditions so that when the same conditions recur in the body they impel the soul to the same thought; and conversely when the same thought recurs, it disposes the body to return to the same conditions.[9]

On Loeb's view, then, the fact that soul and body are of such diverse natures was not, for Descartes, even a presumptive barrier to their entering into the most intimate of causal relations. It seems to me that this reply might be effective as a

---

8. Louis E. Loeb, *From Descartes to Hume* (Ithaca, NY and London: Cornell University Press, 1981). See pp. 134–49. See also Daniel Garber's "Understanding Interaction: What Descartes Should Have Told Elisabeth," cited in note 5; Eileen O'Neill, "Mind-Body Interaction and Metaphysical Consistency: A Defense of Descartes," 227–45. *Journal of the History of Philosophy* 25 (1987); Marleen Rozemond, *Descartes's Dualism* (Cambridge, MA: Harvard University Press, 1998).

9. *Descartes' Philosophical Letters*, trans. and ed. Anthony Kenny (Oxford: Oxford University Press, 1963), p. 210. I am doubtful as to whether this passage supports Loeb's Humean reading of Descartes, for Descartes is using here causal verbs like "impel" and "dispose" to describe the regularities.

first pass—as a challenge to the critics of Descartes like Kenny
to put up a real argument or shut up. Why can't Descartes just
say that causation, at least on some fundamental level, is a
brute fact based solely on regularities governing events, and
that there is compelling evidence, in the form of the countless
mind-body correlations familiar from everyday experience, for
the reality of mind-body causation? But does it help Descartes
to turn him into a proto-Humean "constant conjunctionist"
on causation? I don't think it does, and the reason is simple to
see and also instructive. It can be seen that Descartes's trouble
with mental causation has nothing to do with the bruteness or
primitiveness of causation or whether causation is merely a
matter of Humean regularity, and that it has everything to do
with the supposed nonspatiality of Cartesian minds.

Suppose that two persons, Smith and Jones, are "psychophysically synchronized," as it were, in such a way that each
time Smith's mind wills to raise his hand, Jones's mind also wills
to raise his (Jones's) hand, and every time they will to raise
their hands, their hands rise. There is a constant conjunction
between Smith's mind's willing to raise a hand and Smith's
hand's rising, and, similarly, between Jones's mind's willing to
raise a hand and Jones's hand's going up. If you are a constant
conjunctionist about causation, this would suffice for saying
that a given instance of Smith's willing to raise a hand is a cause
of the subsequent rising of his hand, and similarly in the case of
Jones. But there is a problem. For we see that instances of
Smith's mind's willing to raise a hand are constantly conjoined
not only with his hand's rising but *also with Jones's hand's rising*,
and, similarly, instances of Jones's mind's willing to raise a hand
are constantly conjoined with Smith's hand's rising. So why is it
not the case that Smith's volition causes Jones's hand to go up,
and that Jones's volition causes Smith's hand to go up?

It will not do to say that after all Smith wills *his* hand to rise
and that's why his willing causes his hand, not Jones's hand, to
rise. It isn't clear what this reply can accomplish, but it begs

the question on hand. The reason is that what makes Smith's hand Smith's, not Jones's, that is, what makes Smith's body the body with which Smith's mind is "united," is the fact that there is specially intimate and direct causal commerce between the two. To say that this is the body with which this mind is united is to say that this body is the only material thing that this mind can *directly* affect—that is, without anything else serving as a causal intermediary—and that all changes this mind can cause in other bodies are via changes in this body, changes directly caused by this mind. This is *my* body, and this is *my* arm, because they are things that I can move without moving any other body. I can raise *your* arm only by grabbing it with my hand and pulling it up.[10] And something similar must obtain for body-to-mind causation as well. The "union" of a mind and a body that Descartes speaks of, therefore, presupposes mental causation. Whether or not this is a historically correct reading of Descartes, a causal account of "ownership" seems the most natural option for substance dualists, and I do not know of noncausal alternatives that make any real sense.

I have heard some people say that we could simply take the concept of the mind's "union" with a body as an unexplained and unexplainable primitive,[11] and that it is simply a primitive fact, perhaps divinely ordained,[12] that this mind and this body are merged in a proper union that is a person. I find such an

10. Does this exclude telekinesis? Yes. That probably is the main reason why there is something a priori strange about telekinesis. If telekinesis were a widely spread everyday phenomenon, that might very well undermine the idea that each of us has a distinct body.

11. According to Daniel Garber, something like this was Descartes's view; in addition, Descartes claimed the notion to be intelligible in its own right; see Garber's "Understanding Interaction: What Descartes Should Have Told Elisabeth."

12. For an unabashedly theistic approach of this kind, see John Foster, "A Brief Defense of the Cartesian View," in *Soul, Body, and Survival*, ed. Kevin Corcoran (Ithaca, NY: Cornell University Press, 2001), p. 29.

approach inadequate and unsatisfying. For it concedes that the notion of "union" of a mind and a body, and hence the notion of a person, is unintelligible. For what is it for an immaterial thing wholly outside space to be "united" or "joined" with a material body with a specific location in space? The word "united" merely gives a name to a mystery rather than clarifying it. If God chose to unite my body with my mind, just what is it that he did? I am not asking *why* he chose to unite this particular mind with this particular body, or *why* he decided to engage in such activities as uniting minds and bodies, or *whether* he, or anyone else, could have powers to do things like that. All of that could remain a mystery and I wouldn't complain. What I am asking for is more basic: If God "united" my mind and my body to make a person, there must be a relationship R such that a mind stands in relation R to a body if and only if that mind and that body constitute a unitary person. In uniting my mind and my body, God related the two with R. Unless we know what R is, we do not know what it is that God wrought. The word "union" remains a mere label, and we do not understand what it is that the theistic explanation is attempting to explain when it says that God ordained the "union."

CAUSATION AND THE "PAIRING" PROBLEM

The difficulty we have seen with Loeb's interpretation of Descartes as a Humean in matters of causation, I believe, points to a more fundamental difficulty in the idea that mental substances, outside physical space, can enter into causal relations with objects in physical space. What is perhaps more surprising, the very same difficulty besets the idea that such nonspatial mental substances can enter into any sort of causal relations, whether with material substances or *with other mental substances.*

Let us begin with a simple example of physical causation: two guns, A and B, are simultaneously fired, and this results in the simultaneous death of two persons, Adam and Bob. What makes it the case that the firing of A caused Adam's death and the firing of B caused Bob's death, and not the other way around? What are the principles that underlie the correct and incorrect *pairings* of cause and effect in a situation like this? We can call this "the causal pairing problem," or "the pairing problem" for short.[13]

Two possible ways for handling this problem come to mind. (1) We can trace a continuous causal chain from the firing of A to Adam's death, and another such chain from the firing of B to Bob's death. (In fact, we can, with a high-speed camera, trace the bullet's trajectory from gun A to Adam and similarly for gun B and Bob.) No causal chain exists from the firing of A to Bob's death, or from the firing of B to Adam's death. (2) We look for a "pairing relation", *R*, that holds between A's firing and Adam's death and between B's firing and Bob's death, but not between A's firing and Bob's death or B's firing and Adam's death. In this particular case, when the two guns were fired, gun A, not gun B, was located at an appropriate distance from Adam and pointed in his direction, and similarly with gun B and Bob. It is these *spatial relations* (distance, orientation, etc.) that help pair the firing of A with Adam's death and the firing of B with Bob's death. Spatial relations seem to serve as the "pairing relations" in this case, and perhaps for all cases of physical causation involving distinct objects.

The two methods may be related, but let us set aside this question for now.

Turn now to a situation involving nonphysical Cartesian souls as causal agents. There are two souls, A and B, and they perform an identical mental act at time *t*, as a result of which a change occurs in material substance M shortly after *t*. We may

13. The "pairing problem" was first formulated by John Foster in "Psycho-physical Causal Relations," *American Philosophical Quarterly* 5 (1968): 64–70. See also Foster's *The Immaterial Self* (London: Routledge, 1991). I earlier discussed this problem in "Causation, Nomic Subsumption, and the Concept of Event," *Journal of Philosophy* 70 (1973): 217–36.

suppose that mental actions of the kind involved generally cause physical changes of the sort that happened in M, and, moreover, that in the present case it is soul A's action, not soul B's, that caused the change in M. Surely, such a possibility must exist. But ask: What relation might serve to pair soul A's action with the change in M, a relation that is absent in the case of soul B's action and the change in M? That is, what could be the pairing relation in this case? Evidently, no spatial relations can be invoked to answer this question, for souls are not in space and are not able to bear spatial relations to material things. Soul A cannot be any "nearer" to material object M, or more propitiously "oriented" in relation to it, than soul B is. Is there anything that can do for souls what space, or a network of spatial relations, does for material things?

But what about mind-to-mind causation? Would this be any easier for Descartes? Consider a purely mental world, a world inhabited only by Cartesian souls; such a world must be possible, since souls are "substances," that is, independent existents. Soul A acts in a certain way and so does soul B at the same time. This is followed by certain changes in two other souls, A* and B*. Suppose that actions of A and B are causes of the changes in A* and B*. But which cause caused which effect? If we want a solution that is analogous to case (2) above for the firings of guns and the deaths, what we need is a pairing relation R such that R holds, say, for A and A*, and for B and B*, but not for A and B*, or for B and A*. Since these entities are immaterial souls outside physical space, R cannot be, or include, a spatial relation, or any other kind of physical property or relation. The radical nonspatiality of mental substances rules out the possibility of invoking spatial relationships to ground cause-effect pairings.

Evidently, then, the pairing relation R must be some kind of psychological relation. But what could that be? Could R be some kind of intentional relation, such as thinking of, picking out, and referring to? Perhaps, soul A gazes at souls A* and B*, and singles out A*, and causes a change in it. But how do we understand these relations like gazing at and picking out? What is it for A to pick out A* rather than B*? To pick out some concrete thing outside us, we must be in a certain cognitive relation to it; we must perceive it somehow and be able to single it out from other things near and around it—that is, perceptually identify it. Take perception: What is it for me to perceive this tree, not another tree which is hidden behind it and which is qualitatively indistinguishable from it? The only credible answer we have is the familiar causal account, according to which the tree that I perceive is the one that is causing my perceptual experience as of a tree, and I do not see the hidden tree because it bears no causal relation to my perceptual experience.[14] Ultimately, these intentional relations must be explained on the basis of causal relations (this is not to say that they are wholly analyzable in terms of causality), and this means that we cannot explain what it is for soul A to pick out soul A* rather than B* except by positing some kind of causal relation that holds for A and A* but not for A and B*. If this is right, invoking intentional relations to do causal pairings begs the question: we need causal relations to understand intentionality. Even if intentional relations were free of causal involvements, that would not by itself show that they would suffice as pairing relations. In addition, they must satisfy certain structural requirements; as will become clear as we proceed, they must suffice for the individuation of intentional objects, and it is by no means clear that intentional relations can satisfy these requirements.

We are not necessarily supposing that one single R will suffice for all causal relations between two mental substances. But if the physical case is any guide, we seem to be in need of a

---

14. This of course is the causal theory of perception. See H. P. Grice, "The Causal Theory of Perception," *Proceedings of the Aristotelian Society*, supplementary vol. 35 (1961).

certain kind of "space," not physical space of course, but some kind of a nonphysical coordinate system that gives every mental substance and every event involving a mental substance a *unique location* (at a time), and which yields for each pair of mental entities a determinate relationship defined by their "locations" (analogous to the distance-orientation relation between a pair of spatial objects). Such a system of "mental space" could provide us with a basis for a solution to the pairing problem, and enable us to make sense of causal relations between nonspatial mental entities. But I don't think we have any idea what such a framework might look like—what purely psychological relations might generate such a space-like structure. I don't think we have any idea where to begin.

What about using the notion of causal chain to connect the souls in the right cause-effect relationships? Can there be a causal chain between soul A's action and the change in soul A*, and between soul B's action and the change in soul B*? But do we have any understanding of such purely mental causal chains? What could such chains be like outside physical space? Hume required that a pair of causally connected events that are spatiotemporally separated be connected by a chain of *spatially contiguous* events. It is difficult to imagine what kind of causal chain might be inserted between events involving two mental substances. Presumably we have to place a third soul, C, between soul A and soul A*, such that A's action causes a change in C which in turn causes the change in A*. But what could "between" mean here? What is it for an immaterial and nonspatial thing to be "between" two other immaterial and nonspatial things? In the physical case, it is physical space that gives a sense to betweenness. In the mental case, what could serve the role that space serves in the physical case?

One might say: For soul C to be "between" souls A and A* in a sense relevant to present purposes is for A's action to cause a change in C and for this change to cause a change in A*. That is, betweenness is to be taken as causal betweenness.

This of course is the idea of a causal chain, but it is clear that this idea does not give us an independent handle on the pairing problem. The reason is easy to see: it begs the question. Our original question was: How do we pair soul A's action with a change in soul A*? Now we have two pairing problems instead of one: First, we need to pair soul A's action with a change in a third soul, C, and then we need to pair this change in C with the change in A*. This means that the two methods above, (1) and (2), for cause-effect paring, are not independent, and this for a very simple reason: the very idea of a causal chain makes sense only if an appropriate notion of causation is already in hand, and this requires a prior solution to the pairing problem. It follows that method (2) is the only way to effect cause-effect pairings.

We are, therefore, back with (2)—that is, with the question of what psychological relations might serve the role that spatial relations serve in the case of physical causation. The problem here is independent of the Humean constant conjunction view of causation, and therefore independent of the difficulty we raised for Loeb's defense of Descartes.[15] For suppose that there is a "necessary," counterfactual-sustaining regularity connecting properties F and G of immaterial mental substances. A mental substance A has F at t, and an instant later, at t^*, two mental substances, B and C, which share identical intrinsic properties, acquire property G. I think we must countenance the following to be a possible situation: A's having F at t causes B to have G at t^*, but it does not cause C to have G at t^*. Suppose it is claimed that what distinguishes the two cases is that

15. As can be seen by reflecting on the case discussed earlier of Smith and Jones who are "psychophysically synchronized," the pairing problem arises even at the level of stating Humean constant conjunctions. So, even if we make Descartes into a Humean, as Loeb suggests, this would not help Descartes to escape the pairing problem. More broadly, my arguments do not depend on the use of a heavy-duty concept of causation, as has been suggested by some writers.

the counterfactual "If A had not had F at t, B would not have had G at t^*" is true, whereas the counterfactual "If A had not had F at t, C would not have had G at t^*" is false. Well and good. But if that is the case, there must be an intelligible and principled account of why the first counterfactual is true and the second false. I do not believe we could simply assert this as a brute fact for which no explanation is possible or needed and leave it at that. Since B and C are intrinsically alike, the difference in the truth-values of the two counterfactuals must be on account of some relation R that A bears to B but not to C. What could this relation be? Cases like this are not outré examples made up for philosophical argument; such situations should be perfectly ordinary ones in a Cartesian world. If so, how would we ascertain causal relationships in such a world?

If these reflections are essentially right, our idea of causation requires that the causally connected items be situated in a space-like framework. It has been widely believed, as we noted, that Cartesian dualism of two substances runs into insurmountable difficulties in explaining the possibility of causal relations across the two domains, mind to body and body to mind—especially, the former. But what our considerations show is that the problem runs deeper: the very same difficulties beset substantival dualism in regard to the possibility of mental-to-mental causation. Under substance dualism, mind-to-mind causation is no more intelligible than mind-to-body causation. Furthermore, the difficulty is rooted deep in the nature of immaterial minds: it is their supposed essential nonspatiality that makes it impossible for them to meet a basic requirement of causality, namely the need for pairing relations. Perhaps, Leibniz was wise to renounce all causal relations between individual substances, or monads—although I have no idea as to his actual reasons for this doctrine. A purely Cartesian world seems like a pretty lonely place, inhabited by immaterial souls each of which is an island unto itself, totally isolated from all other souls. Even the actual world, if we are immaterial souls, would be a lonely place for us; each of us, as an immaterial entity, would be entirely cut off from anything else, whether physical or nonphysical, in our surroundings. Can you imagine any existence lonelier than an immaterial self?

CAUSALITY AND SPACE

The plausible fact that the causal pairing problem for physical causation is solved by invoking spatial relations tells us something important about causation and the physical domain. By locating each and every physical item—object and event—in an all-encompassing coordinate system, the framework of physical space imposes a determinate relation on every pair of items in that domain. Causal structure of the physical domain presupposes this spatial (or more broadly, spacetime) framework. Causal relations must be selective and discriminating, in the sense that there can be two objects with identical intrinsic properties such that a third object causally acts on one but not the other, and, similarly, that there can be two intrinsically indiscernible objects such that one of them, but not the other, causally acts on a third object. We believe that objects with identical intrinsic properties must have the same causal powers or potentials, both active and passive (some would identify the causal powers of an object with the set of its intrinsic properties). However, objects with the same causal powers can differ in the exercise, or manifestation, of their powers, vis-à-vis other objects around them. This calls for a principled way of distinguishing intrinsically indiscernible objects in causal situations, and it is plausible that spatial relations provide us with the principal means for doing this. Prima facie, spatial relations have the right sorts of properties; for example, causal influences generally diminish as distance increases, and barriers of various sorts can be set up in the right places in space to prevent or impede propagation of causal influences (though not of gravity, we are told). In general, causal relations between physical objects or events appear to depend crucially on their spatiotemporal relations to each other; think about the point of establishing alibis—"I wasn't there," if true, can be sufficient for "I didn't do it." To avoid being burned in a fire, you run away from it as fast as you can—that is, you try to put as much distance as you can between you and the fire. The temporal order alone will not be sufficient as a causal framework; for there can be two or more contemporaneous objects with identical intrinsic properties whose causal behaviors are different. We need a full spacetime framework for this purpose. It was not for nothing that Hume included "contiguity" in space and time, as well as constant conjunction and temporal precedence, among his conditions for causal relations. From our present perspective, Hume's contiguity condition— or the condition that a spatially separated cause-effect be connected by a chain of contiguous cause-effect pairs—can be seen as his solution to the pairing problem. It is also what makes Humean causation an essentially spatial concept. Outside physical space, Humean causation makes no sense. It seems to me that the significance and importance of this condition for Hume's account of causation has not been properly understood or appreciated.

If this is right, it gives us one plausible way of vindicating the critics of Descartes who, as we saw, argued that the radically diverse natures of mental and material substances preclude causal relations between them. It is of the essence of material substances that they have determinate positions in spacetime and that there be a determinate spatiotemporal relationship between each pair of them.[16] Descartes of course talked of extendedness in space as the essence of matter, but we

16. At least on the classic conception of spacetime.

can broadly construe this to include other spatial properties and relations for material substances. Now consider the mental side: As I take it, the Cartesian doctrine has it that it is part of the souls' essential nature that they are wholly outside the spatial order and lack all spatial properties. And it is this essential nonspatiality that makes trouble for their participation in causal relations. As earlier noted, it isn't just mind-to-body causation, but also mind-to-mind causation, that is imperiled by the nonspatiality of immaterial minds.

We have already seen how difficulties arise for mind-to-body and mind-to-mind causation. Unsurprisingly, body-to-mind causation fares no better. The details are similar and can be skipped. But let us note that given that we had trouble envisioning a system of pairing relations for the domain of mental substances, it seems out of the question that we could generate a system that would work across the divide between the mental and material realms. If this is true, not even epiphenomenalism is an option for the serious substance dualist.

I am of course not claiming that these considerations are what motivated the long line of critics of Descartes's interactionism. I am only suggesting a way of fleshing out their worries and showing that there is indeed a concrete basis for these worries. It turns out that, as Kenny and others have said, causal interaction between mind and matter is precluded by their diverse natures, and we have identified the essential diversity that matters, namely the spatiality of bodies and the supposed nonspatiality of minds.

"Affinity" does turn out to make a difference for causation after all. Causality requires pairing relations, and this diversity between minds and bodies does not permit such relations for minds and bodies. What the critics perhaps didn't see was the possibility that the same difficulty bedevils causal relations within the realm of the minds as well. If all this is right, there is no need to appeal to the alleged "mechanical" nature of material causation and the supposed teleological or rational character of mental causation to show that mind-body causation is problematic. An effective argument can be formulated at a more general and basic level.

WHY NOT LOCATE SOULS IN SPACE?

These reflections might lead one to wonder whether it would help the cause of dualist causation if immaterial minds were brought into space and given locations in it, not as extended substances like material bodies but as extensionless points. After all, Descartes spoke of the pineal gland as "the seat" of the soul, and it is easy to find passages in his writings that seem to give souls positions in space. And most people, philosophers included, who believe in souls appear to think that our souls are somehow located inside our bodies—my soul in my body and your soul in your body. It seems to me that the thinking here is closely associated with the idea that my soul is in direct causal contact with my body and your soul with your body. The pineal gland is the seat of the soul for Descartes only because it is where unmediated mind-body causal interaction is thought to take place. This confirms my general feeling that mind-body causation generates pressures to bring minds somehow into space, which, for Descartes, is exclusively the realm of matter.

In any case, putting souls into physical space may create more problems than solve them. For one thing, we need a motivated way of locating each soul at a particular point in space. Leibniz said that we locate the soul in a body but we don't think it is at some particular place within it:

> The second [mode of being somewhere] is the *definitive*. In this case, one can "define"—i.e. determine—that the located thing lies within a given space without being able to specify exact points or places which it occupies exclusively. That is how some people have thought that the soul is in the body, because they have not thought it possible to specify an exact point such

that the soul or something pertaining to it is there and at no other point. Many competent people still take that view.[17]

But does this make any sense? If my soul, as a geometric point, is in my body, it must be either in the top half of my body or its bottom half. If it's in the top half, it must be either in its left or right half, and so on, and we should be able to corner the soul into as small and specific a region of my body as we like. And why should we locate my soul in my body to begin with? Why can't we locate all the souls of this world in one tiny place, say this pencil holder on my desk, like the many thousand angels dancing on the head of a pin?

It would beg the question to locate my soul where my body, or brain, is on the ground that my soul and my body are in direct causal interaction with each other; the reason is that the possibility of such interaction is what is at issue and we are considering the localizability of souls in order to make mind-body causation possible. Second, if locating souls in space is to help with the pairing problem, it must be the case that no more than one soul can occupy a single spatial point; for otherwise spatial relations would not suffice to uniquely identify each soul in relation to other souls in space. This is analogous to the principle of "impenetrability of matter," a principle whose point can be taken to be the claim that space provides us with a criterion of individuation for material things. This principle says that material objects occupying exactly the same spatial region at one time are one and the same—at least from the causal point of view.[18] What we need is a similar principle

17. Leibniz, *New Essays on Human Understanding*, tr. and ed. Peter Remnant and Jonathan Bennett (Cambridge: Cambridge University Press, 1981), bk. 2, ch. 23, sec. 21.

18. This qualification is in consideration of a fairly widely shared view that there are counterexamples ("coincident objects") to the principle that material objects are individuated by spatial coincidence; e.g., a statue and the lump of bronze that "constitutes" it. But then there are philosophers, e.g., Lynne Rudder Baker, who hold—implausibly, in my opinion—that these spatially coincident objects can, and do, have different causal powers.

for souls, that is, a principle of "impenetrability of souls": Two distinct souls cannot occupy exactly the same point in space at the same time. But if souls are subject to spatial exclusion, in addition to the fact that the exercise of their causal powers are constrained by spatial relations, why aren't souls just material objects, albeit of a very special, and strange, kind? Moreover, there is a prior question: Why should we think that a principle of spatial exclusion applies to immaterial souls? To solve the pairing problem for souls by placing them in space we need such a principle, but that is not a reason for thinking that the principle is true. We cannot wish it into truth—we need independent reasons and evidence.

Moreover, if a soul, all of it, is at a geometric point, it is puzzling how it could have enough structure to account for all the marvelous causal work it is supposed to perform and how one might explain the differences between souls in regard to their causal powers. You may say: A soul's causal powers arise from its mental structure, and mental structure doesn't take up space. But what is mental structure? What are its parts and how are the parts configured in a structure? If a soul's mental structure is to account for its distinctive causal powers, then, given the pairing problem and the essentiality of spatial relations for causation, it is unclear how a wholly nonspatial mental structure could account for a soul's causal powers. To go on: If souls exclude each other for spatial occupancy, do they exclude material bodies as well? If not, why not? It may be that one's dualist commitments dictate certain answers to these questions. But that would hardly show they are the "correct" answers. When we think of the myriad questions and puzzles that arise from locating souls in physical space, it is difficult to escape the conclusion that whatever answers might be offered to these questions would likely look ad hoc and fail to convince. Locating souls in space, therefore, is not an option that is going to help the dualist cause, and Descartes was wise to keep them out of it.

Concluding Remarks

I have tried to explore considerations that seem to show that the causal relation indeed exerts a strong pressure toward a degree of homogeneity over its domain, and, moreover, that the kind of homogeneity it requires includes, at a minimum, spatiotemporality, which arguably entails physicality. The more we think about causation, the clearer becomes our realization that the possibility of causation between distinct objects depends on a shared space-like coordinate system in which these objects are located, a scheme that individuates objects by their "locations" in the scheme. Are there such schemes other than physical space? I don't believe we know of any. This alone makes trouble for serious substance dualisms and dualist conceptions of what it is to be a person—unless, like Leibniz, you are prepared to give up causal relations altogether. Malebranche denied causal relations between all finite substances, reserving causal powers exclusively for God, whom he regarded as the only genuine causal agent that exists. It is perhaps not surprising that among the dualists of his time, Descartes was the only major philosopher who chose to include minds as an integral part of the causal structure of the world. In defense of Descartes, we can ask: What would be the point of having souls as immaterial substances if they turn out to have no causal powers, not even powers to be affected by things around them? It is all too easy to excoriate Descartes for his unworkable metaphysics; I believe we should applaud him for showing a healthy respect for commonsense in defending mental causation and in persevering to make sense of our intuitive dualist conception of what it is to be a person. It appears that for many of Descartes's contemporaries, substance dualism was more important than mental causation; Descartes tried to have both and got himself in deep trouble. It seems that at that point in time it didn't occur to most philosophers to blame the trouble on substance dualism and keep mental causation.

What we must conclude, therefore, is that substance dualism offers little hope for mitigating our difficulties with mental causation. Our considerations show that the very idea of immaterial, nonspatial entities precludes them from entering into causal relations; in fact, I think that the very idea of such objects may well be incoherent and unintelligible. In the preceding two chapters we saw that property dualism, of which nonreductive physicalism is the most influential contemporary form, encounters deep difficulties with mental causation. We have now seen that substance dualism fares no better. Our overall provisional conclusion has to be that no form of dualism, whether substance or property dualism, can serve as a basis for explaining how it is possible for our mentality to be so deeply enmeshed in the causal network of the physical world. For it seems beyond doubt that mentality is part of the causal structure of the world and appears seamlessly integrated into it.[19]

19. This chapter is descended from a paper first presented at a conference on mind-body dualism at University of Notre Dame in March, 1998. See Timothy O'Connor's reply, "Causality, Mind, and Free Will," in *Soul, Body and Survival*, ed. Kevin Corcoran (Ithaca, NY: Cornell University Press, 2001). For further discussion, see Noa Latham, "Substance Physicalism," in *Physicalism and Its Discontents*, ed. Carl Gillett and Barry Loewer (Cambridge: Cambridge University Press, 2001.

4

Reduction, Reductive Explanation, and Closing the "Gap"

IT IS NOT A matter of dispute that mental phenomena are intimately correlated with physical events, and, so far as we know, neural events in the brain are the physical correlates of mental events. Often one speaks of the neural "substrates" of mental states, suggesting that there is here a dependency relationship between the mental and the neural that goes beyond mere correlation. Mind-body supervenience as it is standardly understood captures this idea: mental phenomena not only correlate with neural processes but their existence and occurrence are contingent on the presence of appropriate processes in the brain. Some prefer to say that mental phenomena are "emergent phenomena" arising from neural processes. Whichever idiom you prefer, there is this question to ponder: Why does pain correlate with, depend on, or emerge from C-fiber stimulation? Why doesn't it correlate, etc. with a neural state of another kind? Why doesn't itch or tickle arise from C-fiber stimulation? Why does any conscious experience arise from neural states like C-fiber stimulation?

Answering these and related questions constitutes the problem of the "explanatory gap," a by-now familiar term introduced by Joseph Levine in 1983;[1] it is what David Chalmers

---

1. Joseph Levine, "Materialism and Qualia: The Explanatory Gap," *Pacific Philosophical Quarterly* 64 (1983): 354–61.

has called the "hard problem" of consciousness.[2] But the problem goes further back, at least to T. H. Huxley in 1866,[3] William James in 1890,[4] and the British emergentists of the early twenteith century. It is called an explanatory gap because it evidently calls for an explanation of why pain, not itch or tickle, arises out of C-fiber stimulation, and why and how conscious experience arises from neural states. But it is also a predictive, or epistemic, gap: as the emergentists claimed, it seems possible for us to know all about the physiology of a creature, say Thomas Nagel's famously inscrutable bats,[5] but have no idea of the qualitative character of its inner experience. Prima facie, an unbridgeable gap seems to exist, separating even the most complete and perfect knowledge of the brain as a biological/physical system from knowledge of the conscious experiences that may be going on in that brain.

Exactly what needs to be done to close this gap? Two ideas have often been mentioned for closing the gap, and these are reduction and reductive explanation. The thought is that if we could *reduce* pain to C-fiber stimulation, or *reductively explain* pain in terms of a neural state, that would suffice to eliminate the gap. But what is reduction and what is reductive explanation? And how do they manage to close the gap? These are among the questions we will be taking up here.

2. David Chalmers, *The Conscious Mind* (Oxford and New York: Oxford University Press, 1996).

3. T. H. Huxley wrote: "But what consciousness is, we know not; and how it is that anything so remarkable as a state of consciousness comes about as the result of irritating nervous tissue is just as unaccountable as the appearance of the Djin when Aladdin rubbed his lamp in the story, or as any other ultimate fact of nature"; *Lessons in Elementary Physiology* (London: The Macmillan Co., 1866). (I owe this reference to Güven Güzeldere's introduction ["The Many Faces of Consciousness: A Field Guide"] to *The Nature of Consciousness*, ed. Ned Block, Güven Güzeldere, and Owen Flanagan (Cambridge, MA: MIT Press, 1997).

4. See chapter 1.

5. Thomas Nagel, "What Is It Like To Be a Bat?" *Philosophical Review* 83 (1974): 435–50.

REDUCTION AND REDUCTIVE EXPLANATION

As everyone knows, reduction and reductionism have had a rough time of it for several decades. Reductive explanation, however, has been spared the ill repute of reduction. In fact, philosophers who are proud and sworn enemies of reduction seem to have only nice things to say about reductive explanation. They regard it as a viable enterprise of great importance, scientifically and philosophically, even where reduction has been precluded as a possibility.

Since around the mid-century, reductionism in many areas has seemed to many like an unsophisticated and naively overreaching doctrine, and reductions have come to be viewed as making unrealistic and unattainable demands, both philosophically and scientifically. In contrast, reductive explanation has a kinder and gentler ring to it, and seems not to be burdened with the impossible metaphysical demands that reduction seems to force upon us. To do justice to our physicalist inclinations and the pervasive and highly successful micro-oriented research strategies in the sciences, why isn't it enough to require that the phenomena of the world are *reductively explainable* in physical terms? Reductive explanation, unlike reduction, could safeguard the ontological autonomy of higher-level, nonphysical phenomena. Explaining a phenomenon seems in no way to damage or diminish its ontological status, whereas reducing it strikes us as undermining its standing as a genuine existent. And if all phenomena are physically explainable, why isn't that good enough for physicalism?

Jerry Fodor's 1974 paper, "Special Sciences," has often been credited, and rightly so, for having had a major hand in turning the tide against reductionist physicalism. It is interesting to see, however, that in the midst of his relentless argument against reductionism, Fodor takes a brief pause to throw off these seldom noticed obiter dicta:

> It seems to me (to put the point quite generally) that the classical construal of the unity of science has really badly misconstrued the

goal of scientific reduction. The point of reduction is *not* primarily to find some natural kind predicate of physics coextensive with each kind predicate of a special science. *It is, rather, to explicate the physical mechanisms whereby events conform to the laws of the special sciences.* I have been arguing that there is no logical or epistemological reason why success in the second of these projects should require success in the first, and that the two are likely to come apart *in fact* wherever the physical mechanisms whereby events conform to a law of the special sciences are heterogeneous.[6]

Finding for each special science predicate a nomologically coextensive predicate of physics would generate enough "bridge laws" connecting the proprietary vocabularies of the two sciences to enable a Nagelian derivational reduction of the former to the latter. But the phenomenon of multiple realization, which Fodor and others have taken to be pervasive for special science properties, makes these bridge laws unavailable. Hence, there can be no reduction of the special sciences, including psychology, and no reduction of higher-level special science properties. However, this does not preclude, Fodor is suggesting, the possibility of explaining special science phenomena and laws in terms of their underlying physical mechanisms.[7] In fact, Fodor is recommending that reduction be replaced by reductive explanation as the goal of micro-oriented scientific research. Unfortunately, though, Fodor says nothing further about reductive explanation in "Special Sciences," making it difficult to assess his claim that reductive explanation in terms of "physical mechanisms" can thrive even where reduction

6. Jerry Fodor, "Special Sciences, or the Disunity of Science as a Working Hypothesis," in *Readings in Philosophy of Psychology*, vol. 1, ed. Ned Block (Cambridge, MA: Harvard University Press, 1980), p. 127 (emphasis added). Originally published in 1974.

7. Fodor's enthusiasm for implementing physical mechanisms for higher-level phenomena, including psychological phenomena, has not diminished; see, e.g., his "Making Mind Matter More," in *A Theory of Content and Other Essays* (Cambridge, MA: MIT Press, 1990).

fails, and that it is good enough to serve the purposes for which others had sought reductions.

An approach of this kind appears to be shared by more than a few philosophers working in this area. Although they are against the possibility of reduction, in particular mind-body reduction, their allegiance to physicalism shows itself in their assumption that psychological phenomena—psychological capacities, functions, and activities—are grounded in underlying physical mechanisms. If the brain is not the seat of our souls, as Descartes said, it continues, for contemporary antireductionists, to be the seat of our mentality,[8] and as physicalists we should expect to find in the brain the mechanisms that drive our psychology. David Chalmers, for example, embraces this approach as his starting point. Like Fodor, he thinks that while multiple realization may well rule out reduction, this doesn't mean that it rules out reductive explanation. In *The Conscious Mind*, he makes his position explicit:

> In a certain sense, phenomena that can be realized in many different physical substrates—learning, for example—might not be reducible in that we cannot *identify* learning with any specific lower-level phenomena. But this multiple realizability does not stand in the way of reductively *explaining* any instance of learning in terms of lower-level phenomena.[9]

The idea of reductive explanation is at the core of Chalmers's argument for an antiphysicalist view of consciousness. According to him, we cannot reductively explain consciousness in physical terms any more than we can reduce it. This means, for Chalmers, that consciousness cannot be accommodated within a physicalist scheme, and hence that physicalism is false.

---

8. Note the wonderful title of Paul Churchland's book, *The Engine of Reason, the Seat of the Soul: A Philosophical Journey into the Brain* (Cambridge, MA: MIT Press, 1996). Churchland of course is a reductionist.

9. David Chalmers, *The Conscious Mind*, p. 43. Emphasis in the original.

This raises a host of questions. How does reductive explanation work, and what is it about reductive explanation that makes it invulnerable to the multiple realization, and other antireductionist, arguments? How does reductive explanation differ from plain ordinary explanation? And can we really separate reductive explanation from reduction?

BRIDGE-LAW REDUCTION AND FUNCTIONAL REDUCTION

Before we get to the specific issues, I want to set the stage with a brief review of the general issue of reduction. Recent discussions of reduction and reductionism have been dominated by the classic model of "bridge-law" reduction, developed by Ernest Nagel in the 1950s and '60s.[10] It will be helpful to briefly review this model and see why it does not underwrite a concept of reduction that is appropriate for the purposes of mind-body debates.

Nagel was mainly concerned to model reduction of *theories*, a procedure whereby a scientific theory is reductively absorbed into a more basic theory, and he thought of it as consisting in a logical/mathematical derivation of the laws of the theory targeted for reduction from the laws of the base theory. Since the proprietary vocabularies in which laws of the two theories are couched must be expected to be disjoint, it was thought that to enable the required derivation, auxiliary premises connecting the predicates of the two theories are needed. More specifically, Nagel reduction requires that each primitive predicate, M, of the theory being reduced be connected with a predicate, P, of the base theory in a "bridge law" (or "bridge principle") of the form:

For any $x_1, \ldots, x_n$, $M(x_1, \ldots, x_n)$ if and only if $P(x_1, \ldots, x_n)$

10. See Ernest Nagel, *The Structure of Science* (New York: Harcourt, Brace and World, 1961), ch 11.

These bridge laws, taken to be empirical and contingent, are to serve as auxiliary premises of reductive derivations.[11]

It is easily seen that if this bridge law requirement is met, Nagel reduction of the target theory is guaranteed. For let L be a law of the theory to be reduced; we can use the bridge laws as definitions to rewrite L in the vocabulary of the base theory, turning L into L*, a statement in the language of the base theory. Now, either L* is derivable from the laws of the base theory or it is not. If it is, the derivability condition is met. If it is not, add L* to the base theory as an additional law. This is justified, since L* is expressed purely in the predicates of the base theory and, in missing L*, the original base theory is missing a general truth within its domain. Moreover, adding L* to the theory does not expand its ontological or conceptual resources. This is why bridge laws are the heart of Nagel reduction. It is no wonder then that the availability of bridge laws has been the focus of debate whenever the issue of reducibility is raised.

This model of reduction is beset with grave difficulties, but since I have elaborated on them elsewhere,[12] I will just mention one that is directly pertinent to our present purposes. Briefly, the difficulty is this: By adding the bridge laws to the reductive resources as auxiliary premises, *Nagel reduction essentially extends the reduction base.* If we take reduction to be an explanatory

11. Nagel himself did not require that these laws be biconditionals—that is, that there be a *coextensive* predicate in the reducing theory for each predicate in the higher theory. He only required, at least in his later writings, that *enough* connecting laws (whatever their forms might be) be available to make derivation possible. But, as the quotation from Fodor in the preceding section makes clear, Nagel reduction is standardly interpreted to require that the bridge laws be biconditionals. And there are good reasons for this; see my *Mind in a Physical World* (Cambridge, MA: MIT Press, 1998). In any case, the relevant point is that the Nagel model with this enhanced bridge-law condition has been the standard reference in the debates concerning reductionism.

12. In "Making Sense of Emergence," *Philosophical Studies* 95 (1999): 1–36, and *Mind in a Physical World* (Cambridge, MA: MIT Press/Bradford Books, 1998).

process which yields an explanation of the laws and phenomena being reduced on the basis of the laws of the base theory, Nagel reduction fails to generate such explanations. For, to do so, the reductive derivation must derive the laws being reduced *solely from the explanatory resources available in the base domain*. In a Nagel reduction, however, the bridge laws connecting the two domains enter the picture as indispensable supplementary assumptions, and this means that the base theory has been expanded both in its ideology (via addition of new predicates/concepts) and in its ontology (via addition of new properties). Moreover, these a posteriori bridge laws are now among the basic laws of the expanded base theory. Suppose, as an example, pain correlates with a certain neural state, say, C-fiber stimulation. On a Nagel reduction of pain theory to neurophysiology, then, the pain-Cfs bridge law is an unexplained premise of the derivation of pain laws from laws of neurophysiology. This means that the pain-Cfs correlation law is now one of the axioms of the expanded base theory, and that this new base theory no longer is a pure neurophysiological theory—its primitive predicates include "pain," and among its axioms is a law about pain. But consider the explanatory questions that the emergentists asked—or the questions of the sort that Huxley and James found compelling but unanswerable. What was being demanded was an explanation of why pain correlates with Cfs, to begin with. Why is it that pain arises when Cfs occurs, not when Aδ-fibers are activated? Why doesn't itch or tickle emerge instead? Why does any conscious experience emerge from Cfs? These are precisely requests for explanations of the bridge laws themselves. In using the bridge laws as auxiliary premises of reductive derivations, the Nagelian reductionist is simply assuming exactly what needs to be derived and explained if we are to answer the explanatory questions raised by Huxley, James, and the emergentists—that is, if we are to close the explanatory gap or solve the hard problem of consciousness. A Nagelian bridge-law reduction of psychology to physical/biological theory is something that the emergentists would have gladly acknowledged as a real possibility—in fact, an accomplishable task.[13] It should be clear that a Nagelian reduction of psychology to neurophysiology is simply irrelevant to the issue of reductively explaining psychological phenomena and laws on the basis of neurophysiological laws.

The model of functional reduction which I believe should replace the bridge-law model is intended to remedy the above and other shortcomings of the Nagel model. I will now give a brief description of functional reduction. To reduce a property, say being a gene, on this model, we must first "functionalize" it; that is, we must define, or redefine, it in terms of the causal task the property is to perform. Thus, being a gene may be defined as being a mechanism that encodes and transmits genetic information. That is the first step. Next, we must find the "realizers" of the functionally defined property—that is, properties in the reduction base domain that perform the specified causal task. It turns out that DNA molecules are the mechanisms that perform the task of coding and transmitting genetic information—at least, in terrestrial organisms. Third, we must have an explanatory theory that explains just how the realizers of the property being reduced manage to perform the causal task. In the case of the gene and the DNA molecules, presumably molecular biology is in charge of providing the desired explanations.

For ease of reference, I restate all this in schematic form:

Step 1 [Functionalization of the target property]
Property M to be reduced is given a *functional definition* of the following form:

Having M = def. having some property or other P (in the reduction base domain) such that P performs causal task C.

13. As noted in chapter 1, an obvious and natural proposal at this point is to insist that bridge laws be replaced by property identities. We will be discussing this alternative later in this chapter and the following chapter.

For a functionally defined property M, any property in the base domain that fits the causal specification definitive of M (that is, a property that performs causal task C) is called a "realizer" of M.

> STEP 2 [IDENTIFICATION OF THE REALIZERS OF M]
> Find the properties (or mechanisms) in the reduction base that perform the causal task C.

> STEP 3 [DEVELOPING AN EXPLANATORY THEORY]
> Construct a theory that explains how the realizers of M perform task C.

As I will argue below, it can be seen that unlike Nagelian bridge-law reductions, functional reductions in our sense yield reductive explanations of phenomena involving reduced properties, and that these explanations can satisfy the emergentists' explanatory demands. Moreover, it can be shown that functional reductions also satisfy the emergentists' demand that instantiations of reduced properties be predictable solely on the basis of information concerning phenomena at the base level.

Before moving on, I would like to note the following point: functional reduction as characterized here will, as a rule, proceed in a piecemeal fashion; for it is highly unlikely that we will ever be able to identify, or even be interested in identifying, all the actual and nomologically possible realizers of M. What is more likely is that we would be looking for the realizers of M in a particular population of current interest; for example, the realizers of pain in humans and perhaps other higher mammals. When we have identified pain's realizers in humans, we are entitled to claim that we have reduced human pain to human neurophysiology. Nagel reduction of pain requires an all-or-nothing, one-shot reduction of pain across all organisms, species, and systems. It is clear that functional reduction gives us a more realistic picture of reduction in the sciences.

Explanatory Ascent and Constraint (R)

To return to our main topic, the question is this: What is a reductive explanation and how does it differ from explanations that are not reductive? Emergentists claimed that emergent phenomena are not reductively explainable, or predictable, on the basis of the "basal" conditions from which they emerge. Samuel Alexander, a leading theoretician of British emergentism, urged us to accept the facts of emergence "with natural piety." I believe that when the emergentists claimed emergents to be unexplainable, they had in mind reductive explanation as a distinctive variety of explanation. For emergentists, like C. Lloyd Morgan and C. D. Broad, were well aware that there is an obvious sense in which emergent phenomena are explainable and predictable.[14]

Suppose that pain occurs (in humans) when C-fibers are activated. Given this, we can predict that a person will experience pain on the basis of the evidence that her C-fibers are going to be activated. At the commonsensical level we predict the occurrence of pain, and other mental states, all the time: I see that a fall has caused a bad bruise on your knee and can confidently predict that you are going to experience a severe pain in the knee. But, as Broad would have pointed out,[15] such predictions presuppose in their evidence base prior knowledge of the connection between the emergents and their basal conditions—for example, a correlation between pain and C-fiber activation, or between pain and tissue damage. Consider the following inference:

Whenever someone's C-fibers are stimulated, she experiences pain.

Jones's C-fibers are stimulated at t.

Therefore, she experiences pain at t.

14. C. Lloyd Morgan, *Emergent Evolution* (London: Williams & Norgate, 1923); C. D. Broad, *The Mind and Its Place in Nature* (London: Routledge & Kegan Paul, 1960); first published in 1925.
15. See Broad, *The Mind and Its Place in Nature*, p. 65.

This looks like a perfectly acceptable explanation of why Jones experiences pain at t in terms of her C-fiber being stimulated at t; it has the form of a Hempelian, "deductive-nomological," argument, and it can also serve as a predictive inference to Jones's pain at t on the basis of her neural condition at t. But no one would take it as a *reductive* explanation of Jones's pain in terms of her neurophysiology; nor will it count as an affirmative answer to the emergentist question "Is it possible to infer the occurrences of pain and other conscious states from knowledge of neurophysiology?" We may, with Broad, call predictions of this sort "inductive predictions": from knowledge of past correlations between C-fiber activation and pain, and the knowledge that C-fiber activation will occur, we predict that pain will occur. In contrast, what the emergentists denied was the possibility of what we may call "theoretical prediction" of pain; their claim was that no amount of knowledge about our neural/biological states *alone* will suffice for prediction of pain. To predict pain we must rely on the past observation of pain, in particular the physical conditions under which pain occurs. But such correlations obviously go beyond neurophysiology; they are what Broad calls "trans-ordinal laws," laws that connect phenomena of one order (or level) with those of an adjacent order (or level). In effect, these are the Nagelian bridge laws, laws bridging two levels or domains. It is no surprise, emergentists will say, that you can inductively predict the occurrence of an emergent, since such inductive predictions make use of antecedent knowledge of the conditions under which the emergent phenomenon occurs. For genuine theoretical predictions of emergents, your evidence base is restricted to information *solely* about the base level, the level from which the emergents emerge. To make a theoretical prediction, therefore, we must deduce a statement about the emergent (say, a conscious state) from a set of statements exclusively about the basal level (neural/biological states). And this, the emergentists claimed, cannot be done.[16]

16. See Broad's instructive discussion in *The Mind and Its Place in Nature*, pp. 61–69.

The displayed argument above is disqualified as a reductive explanation for the same reason: the explanans of this explanation makes use of a trans-ordinal law, a law connecting phenomena at different levels, and that is why this explanation does not count as a reductive, or "mechanistic" (as the emergentists would say), explanation of Jones's pain. This should remind us of the failure of Nagel's bridge-law reductions to deliver reductions or reductive explanations. For, as noted, bridge laws are precisely Broad's trans-ordinal laws, and just as the use of bridge laws as auxiliary premises vitiates Nagelian reductions as genuine reductions, the use of trans-ordinal, or emergent, laws in an explanation disqualifies it as a reductive explanation.

If a principled reason is wanted for excluding explanations of this kind as reductive, we can say this: the use of these trans-ordinal laws means that the property whose instantiation is being explained is already part of the ontology of the explanatory theory, and that the concept representing that property is part of the vocabulary of this theory. As we said, the use of such laws expands both the ontology and ideology of the base theory. Consider the above explanation of Jones's pain. Its explanans contains reference to pain, and the theory being invoked to explain this instance of pain already explicitly includes pains, or the property pain, in its ontology, and makes use of the pain-neural correlation as a basic law. This is why this explanation is not a reductive explanation of Jones's pain.

These thoughts point to the following requirement for reductive explanations:

> (R) The explanatory premises of a reductive explanation of a phenomenon involving property F (e.g., an explanation of why F is instantiated on this occasion) must not refer to F.[17]

17. I believe that for most of our present purposes the following weaker constraint will do:

> (R*) The explanatory premises of a reductive explanation of a phenomenon involving property F must not include a law pertaining to F.

We could strengthen (R): Not only must the explanans of a reductive explanation of F not refer to F, but it also must not refer to any other property at the level of F—or, equivalently, a reductive explanation of F may refer in its explanans only to properties at levels lower than that of F. Thus understood, a reductive explanation of pain, for example, would be prohibited from invoking not only pain but also any other conscious states, or perhaps any other mental states.[18]

The idea of reduction, and reductive explanation, involves two distinct domains or levels. To explain a phenomenon simpliciter we may invoke phenomena at the same level, or even those at a higher level, in the explanans. That is the way causal explanations ordinarily work; an event and the cause that is cited to explain it are often at the same level. A window broke because a rock hit it; a billiard ball began moving because another one collided with it; and so on. But a reductive explanation of a phenomenon must be expected to do its job by resorting only to *explanatory resources at a different level*, a "lower" level in relation to the level of the phenomenon to be explained. Why else speak of "reductive" explanation?

Explanation is plausibly regarded as involving logical derivation; at least, logical derivability is the only concrete and objective criterion available in discussions of explainability. To explain a phenomenon we must derive it, or derive a statement representing it, from a set of statements representing its explanans. As is well known, this is a crucial part of the Hempelian deductive-nomological model of explanation, and it is not uncontroversial. However, we will assume in this discussion that

18. Clearly what other states are to be included along with F depends on what we understand by "level." It is equally clear that the individuation of levels is a context-dependent affair; whether, for example, nonphenomenal (e.g., cognitive) mental states are to be allowed in reductive explanation of qualia depends on the nature of the particular reductive project at issue.

explanation is via logical derivation;[19] this is not a point contested in this debate. In any case, if we accept constraint (R), reductive explanation poses a real challenge, and it is this:

How are we to make explanatory ascent from one level to another? Given that explanation is deduction, how is it possible to make a deductive transition from the base level, where our explanatory resources are located, to the higher level, where our explanandum is located?[20]

We may call this "the problem of explanatory ascent." It is the main problem involved in the problem of the explanatory gap: If explanation requires deduction, how can we deductively fill the gap between the explanandum at one level and the purported explanans at another level? To make the problem more concrete: To explain "Jones is experiencing pain" neurophysiologically, we must deduce it from a set of neurophysiological statements about Jones. But the term "pain," or the concept of pain, does not even appear in neurophysiology. So how could we deduce "Jones is experiencing pain" from neurophysiological statements? (Compare Hume's problem of deriving "ought" from "is.") Obviously, some additional help is needed.

There are three presumptive possibilities that might be considered as enablers of explanatory ascent:

(i) Bridge laws, or trans-ordinal laws—contingent, empirical laws connecting explanandum phenomena with phenomena at the reduction base.

19. This of course is not to say that all logical derivations are explanations. For a defense of the view that explanation involves logical derivation, see my "Hempel, Explanation, Metaphysics," *Philosophical Studies* 94 (1999): 1–20.

20. Joseph Levine puts this question as follows: "The problem is this. Given the difference between the vocabularies in which the microfacts and macrofacts are expressed, how do we get a derivation of the latter from the former?" *Purple Haze* (Oxford: Oxford University Press, 2001), p. 64. Levine's answer is the same as mine: There must be conceptual, definitional connections.

(ii) Conceptual connections, e.g., definitions, providing conceptual/semantic relations between the phenomena at the two levels.

(iii) Identity statements that identify the explanandum phenomena with certain lower-level phenomena.[21]

Each of these possibilities must meet the constraint (R) on reductive explanation. This means that we already know that (i) must be ruled out. As we saw, the use of these empirical connecting laws begs the question as far as *reductive* explanation is concerned. So we are down to two possibilities, (ii) and (iii), that is, conceptual connections and identities.

FUNCTIONAL REDUCTION
AND REDUCTIVE EXPLANATION

Chalmers is one of the philosophers who advocate conceptual connections as vehicles of reductive explanations. He writes:

> What is it that allows such diverse phenomena as reproduction, learning, and heat to be reductively explained? In all these cases, the nature of the concepts required to characterize the phenomena is crucial. If someone objected to a cellular explanation of reproduction, "This explains how a cellular process can lead to the production of a complex physical entity that is similar to the original entity, but it doesn't explain reproduction," we would have little patience—for that is all that "reproduction" means. In general, a reductive explanation

21. We will not worry about this statement being a kind of oxymoron, for one could ask how it is possible for anything at *one level* to be identical with something at a *different level*. Levels talk can be interpreted to apply to concepts and languages instead of things in the world. At any rate, there is a pressing need to make the talk of levels more precise.

of a phenomenon is accompanied by some rough-and-ready *analysis* of the phenomenon in question, whether implicit or explicit.[22]

And he evidently believes that explanatory ascent *requires* conceptual connections:

> The point may seem trivial, but the possibility of this kind of analysis undergirds the possibility of reductive explanation in general. Without such an analysis, there would be no explanatory bridge from the lower-level physical facts to the phenomenon in question.[23]

But what form does Chalmers's "conceptual analysis" take? Here is what he says:

> For the most interesting phenomena that require explanation, including phenomena such as reproduction and learning, the relevant notions can usually be analyzed *functionally*. The core of such notions can be characterized in terms of the performance of some function or functions (where "function" is taken causally rather than teleologically), or in terms of the capacity to perform those functions. It follows that once we have explained how those functions are performed, then we have explained the phenomenon in question. Once we have explained how an organism performs the function of producing another organism, we have explained reproduction, for all it means to reproduce is to perform that function.[24]

Joseph Levine, in an earlier paper, takes a similar approach:

> But now how is it that we get an explanation of these superficial properties [observable properties of water] from the chemical theory? Remember, explanation is supposed to involve a

22. *The Conscious Mind*, p. 43.
23. *The Conscious Mind*, p. 44.
24. Ibid.

deductive relation between explanans and explanandum. . . .
For instance, suppose I want to explain why water boils, or
freezes, at the temperatures it does. In order to get an explanation of these facts, we need a definition of "boiling" and "freez-
ing" that brings these terms into the proprietary vocabularies
of the theories appealed to in the explanation.[25]

Both Chalmers and Levine are suggesting, then, that the
reductive explanatory ascent can, and must, be mediated by
definitions, and by definitions they have in mind analytic definitions grounded in conceptual analysis, something that can be
formulated and evaluated a priori.

Chalmers, in the first of the quoted passages, sounds as
though what he has in mind is an explicit definition of the
standard form, for example:

Reproduction = def. organism producing another organism.

But actually what Chalmers and Levine have in mind for definitions is something a little more complicated. Note that
Chalmers talks of "functional analysis" (in the second quoted
passage) and "causal role"; and what Levine calls "explanatory
reduction" below is nothing more or less than the functional
reduction I described earlier:

Notice that on [the view favored by Levine] explanatory reduction is, in a way, a two-stage process. Stage 1 involves the (relatively? quasi?) a priori process of working the concept of the
property to be reduced "into shape" for reduction by identifying the causal role for which we are seeking the underlying
mechanisms. Stage 2 involves the empirical work of discovering just what those underlying mechanisms are.[26]

25. Joseph Levine, "On Leaving Out What It's Like," in *Consciousness*, ed.
Martin Davies and Glyn W. Humphreys (Oxford: Blackwell, 1993), p. 131.
26. "On Leaving Out What It's Like," p. 132. The idea of functional reduction, or functional reductive explanation, though not the terms, can be traced

Levine's two stages correspond exactly to our Steps 1 and 2, and when he talks about definitions, we should take him to be talking about functional definitions, that is, definitions in terms of causal tasks described in a base-level vocabulary.

What does a reductive explanation look like when it uses functional definitions for explanatory ascent? Suppose M is the property for which we seek a reductive explanation; let us suppose that our explanandum is some object, x, having M at t. So we are formulating a reductive explanation of why x has M. Let C be the causal task, or role, defining M. And suppose that x has M on this occasion because x has one of M's realizers, say P_i, on this occasion. A reductive explanation of x's having M at t may look like this:

(I) x has P_i at t.
       P_i satisfies causal role C (in systems like x).
       Having M = def. having some property satisfying causal
       role C.
       Therefore, x has M at t.

Does (I) violate constraint (R) on account of its third line with an occurrence of "M"? The answer is no: the third line is not an explanatory *premise*; it is a definition, and definitions do not count as extra premises of a deduction. Definitions are cheap in proofs; they are free. To put it another way, the third line does not refer to M; it doesn't talk about M. Rather, if it refers to anything, it refers to the concept, or term, M. The above explanation, therefore, does not violate constraint (R). Another point to notice is that this explanatory argument involves an empirical law, the second line, among its explanatory premises, and it can be considered a deductive-nomological explanation in Hempel's sense.

It is also obvious how (I) can be viewed as a predictive argument—a prediction that x will have M at t—exclusively on

---

further back, at least to the writings of David Lewis and David Armstrong in the 1960s.

the basis of lower-level facts, that is, facts at the level of M's realizers. Again, the third line, being a definition, is not a description of a fact involving M.

Suppose pain has been functionalized, say, à la David Armstrong: being in pain is being in a state apt to be caused by tissue damage and apt for causing winces and groans. Why is Jones in pain? Because to be in pain is to be in some state that is apt to be caused by tissue damage and apt for causing winces and groans, and Jones is now in neural state N, which, as it happens, is a state apt to be caused by tissue damage and apt for causing winces and groans. This seems, intuitively, like a perfectly good reductive explanation of Jones's pain, and this explanation is easily converted into a prediction of pain on the basis of facts not involving pain. If this is right, it shows how a functional reduction can close the explanatory gap.

We can also reductively explain why neural state N "correlates" with pain:

(II)   A system, x, is in neural state N at t.
       Neural state N satisfies causal role C (in systems like x).
       Having pain = def. being in some state satisfying causal role C.
       Therefore, x is in pain at t.

One moral to be drawn at this point is that reduction, when understood in terms of the functional model, yields reductive explanation. Moreover, reductive explanations of the type considered here, exemplified in (I) and (II), are possible only if reductions, of the functional kind, are on hand. Evidently this is one point in favor of the functional model of reduction. Earlier we saw Chalmers's claim that even where "reduction" is not available reductive explanation may still be possible. This claim is consistent with our result because by "reduction" he evidently has in mind not functional reduction but type identity reduction of the sort to be discussed in the following section.

KRIPKEAN IDENTITIES AND REDUCTIVE EXPLANATION

But is functional reduction the only way to make a reductive explanatory ascent? A negative position has been forcefully argued by Ned Block and Robert Stalnaker.[27] They agree that a functional reduction, in our sense, is *sufficient* for reductive explanation, but they say it is not the only way. Their point is that a posteriori necessary identities of the kind Kripke has made famous,[28] like "water = H_2O" and "heat is molecular motion," suffice to close the explanatory gap across reductive levels. When we are in a position to avail ourselves of identities like "pain = neural state N," not as a matter of conceptual analysis or definition, but as a posteriori identities, we have in our possession the means for explanatory ascent from neurobiology to phenomenology of experience. Thus, they are proposing (iii) above as another option—actually, the only option, since, according to them, functional definitions of higher-level properties are almost never available. A similar position is defended by Christopher Hill,[29] and Hill and Brian McLaughlin in a critical discussion of Chalmers;[30] however, we will here focus on Block and Stalnaker's arguments.

Here is what Block and Stalnaker say:

> All we reject is the a priori, purely conceptual status attributed to the bridge principles connecting the ordinary description of the

27. Ned Block and Robert Stalnaker, "Conceptual Analysis, Dualism, and the Explanatory Gap," *Philosophical Review* 108 (1999): 1–46.

28. Saul Kripke, *Naming and Necessity* (Cambridge, MA: Harvard University Press, 1980).

29. Christopher Hill, *Sensations* (Cambridge: Cambridge University Press, 1991). We will take up Hill's argument for psychoneural identification in the next chapter.

30. Christopher Hill and Brian McLaughlin, "There Are Fewer Things in Reality Than Are Dreamt of in Chalmers' Philosophy," *Philosophy and Phenomenological Research* 59 (1999): 445–54.

phenomena to be explained with its description in the language of science. What is actually deduced in such an explanation is a description wholly within the language of science of the phenomenon to be explained. For this to answer the original explanatory question, posed in so-called folk vocabulary, all we need to add is the claim that the phenomenon described in scientific language is the same ordinary phenomenon described in a different way. But if the closing of an explanatory gap does not require an a priori deduction of the folk description of the phenomena, then it has not been shown that unavailability of a conceptual analysis of consciousness need be an obstacle to the closing of the explanatory gap between consciousness and the physical.[31]

The following are psychoneural identities of the sort Block and Stalnaker have in mind:

Consciousness = pyramidal cell activity

Pain = C-fiber stimulation

Suppose we want to explain why consciousness ceases in people when they are administered sodium pentothal. From the quoted paragraph above, Block and Stalnaker evidently think that a reductive explanation of this phenomenon could work like this:

(III)   T (neurophysiology)
         An injection of sodium pentothal causes pyramidal cell
         activity to cease (from T).
         (K) Consciousness = pyramidal cell activity.
         Therefore, an injection of sodium pentothal causes loss
         of consciousness.

As I take it, Block and Stalnaker would view this derivation as follows: Neurophysiological theory T logically yields, and explains, the second line. The explanatory activity is finished when the second line has been derived from T. When this explanation is in hand, we are in a position to claim, via the identity (K), that we have explained why an injection of sodium pentothal causes people to lose consciousness. Does (III) comply with constraint (R)? Does the occurrence of "consciousness" in the third line violate the condition that the property for which a reductive explanation is sought not be referred to in any of the explanatory premises? Recall that, on Block and Stalnaker's understanding, the deduction of the explanandum (the last line) from the two preceding lines is not itself part of the explanation. It lies outside the scope of theory T, and it is an extra-theoretical commentary on an explanatory accomplishment within the theory, and this means that (K) is not an explanatory premise. It follows that the use of (K) is in full compliance with constraint (R). All that (K) does in this derivation is to serve as a *rewrite rule*: it allows us to redescribe the phenomenon that has already been explained in another vocabulary—in this instance, the "folk" vocabulary of vernacular psychology.

Unlike definitions based on conceptual analysis, however, Block and Stalnaker's identities are empirical, and one might raise the following concern. Analytic definitions, being a priori and devoid of factual content, are unproblematic as vehicles of reductive derivations; and in so far as a definition "makes" a statement, it is about concepts and expressions, not about things in the world. However, Kripkean identities have rich empirical content; in fact, they apparently entail correlations, and since (R), and also (R*), disallow correlation laws about properties being reduced, we should also disallow stronger statements that imply these correlations. Here a satisfactory reply must be based on a general view about the role of identities in explanation.[32] In any case, there is a point to the objection that we can appreciate when it is recast as an objection to the use of these identities in prediction. That is, these identities, being a posteriori, will not help at all with the emergentists'

32. These issues will be taken up in the next chapter.

question: Can we predict anything about pain or consciousness solely on the basis of our knowledge about its underlying physiological substrate? Making use of Kripkean identities about pain and consciousness in the predictive base will obviously not meet the emergentists' demand. That is to say, these a posteriori identities, whatever they may do for the closing of the explanatory gap, will not help at all in closing the epistemic gap between the brain and consciousness.

Let us turn to another possible explanandum for reductive explanation: *Why is Jones conscious at t?* As far I can tell, all that we can muster on the Block-Stalnaker model is the following:

(IV)   Pyramidal cell activity is going on in Jones's brain at t.

(K) Consciousness = pyramidal cell activity.

Therefore, Jones is conscious at t.

Notice that there is no involvement of neurophysiological theory in this derivation; in particular, (K) cannot be viewed as entailed by neurophysiology—the term "consciousness" does not even appear in that theory. Moreover, the derivation involves no laws, with the identity (K) alone underwriting the deductive transition. But just because (K) is an identity, it seems dubious that it can have any explanatory power of its own. To be sure, like definitions, identities can serve to *mediate* between steps in an explanatory deduction, as we saw in connection with (III); but can they generate, or ground, explanations on their own? When we are struck by "the mystery of consciousness," when the emergentists looked in vain for an understanding of why consciousness emerges from biological processes, or when we ponder the question how a phenomenon like consciousness should, or could, exist in a world that is fundamentally material—that is, when we worry about understanding the phenomenon of consciousness— are the likes of (IV) responsive to our explanatory needs?

At this point, Block and Stalnaker will reply as follows: Identities like (K) should be seen not as helping to answer explanatory questions like "Why is Jones conscious whenever pyramidal cell activity is going on in his brain?" but rather as neutralizing or dissipating them—that is, as showing that *there is nothing here to be explained*. Why is there water just where and when H_2O is present? Why do the two correlate? The appropriate answer here is this: Water just is H_2O, and there is here no correlation to be explained. Why does Hillary Rodham Clinton show up just where and when Chelsea's mother shows up? Again, there is no mysterious correlation to be explained; there is no intelligible question as to how the one "emerges" from the other, or anything of the sort. Just so with consciousness and pyramidal cell activity. Given (K), it no longer makes sense to ask how consciousness emerges out of pyramidal cell activity, not from another sort of neural process, or why there is consciousness just when and where these pyramidal cell activities occur. One is the same as the other, and there is nothing here to explain. Thus, Block and Stalnaker write:

> If we believe that heat is correlated with but not identical to molecular kinetic energy, we should regard as legitimate the question of why the correlation exists and what its mechanism is. But once we realize that heat *is* molecular kinetic energy, questions like this can be seen as wrongheaded.[33]

REMARKS ABOUT BLOCK AND STALNAKER'S PROPOSAL

A good many philosophers, and also scientists, will find these conclusions disappointing. The emergentists' questions about consciousness, about why and how conscious states arise from

---

33. "Conceptual Analysis, Dualism, and the Explanatory Gap," p. 24. For this approach to work, Block and Stalnaker must claim that identities themselves are not open to further explanatory requests (e.g., "Why is pain identical with Cfs?"). Their view is that identities have no explanations. Here is perhaps where the necessity of the Kripkean identities can play a role; for many contingent identities, like "Michael Jordan is the best player on the team," seem to be eminently explainable.

their neural base, are presumptively intelligible questions, they would insist, and any move to show them "improper" or "wrongheaded" should be resisted. These identities don't "close" the explanatory gap; rather, what they show, if they show anything, is that *no such gap exists, or ever existed.* Compare this with how the explanatory gap is handled under the model of functional reduction: recall our earlier examples, (I) and (II), of reductive explanation under the functional model. Unlike Block and Stalnaker's (IV), (I) and (II) do seem to involve an explanatory process; they tell us a reductionist story about why Jones is experiencing pain at *t*, and why pains and C-fiber excitation correlate, without making the explanatory questions illegitimate. Note that both (I) and (II) involve a law as an explanatory premise; a statement to the effect that a given property fills a specified causal role is a general lawlike statement. All this assumes that pain is functionally reducible. If, as is likely, pain is not so reducible, we would just have to accept pain as something whose occurrence is not explainable in terms of the physiological process from which it arises. That is, we would have to accept defeat and acknowledge that there are things in this world that have no explanations.

The main point to note is this: On Block and Stalnaker's account of identity-mediated reduction, even if we have successfully reduced pain to C-fiber stimulation, and consciousness to pyramidal cell activity, that would not yield an explanation, reductive or otherwise, of the occurrence of pain in terms of C-fiber stimulation, or the occurrence of consciousness in terms of pyramidal cell activity. An identity reduction of X to Y does not generate an explanation of the occurrence of X in terms of Y, or Y in terms of X; nor does it enable us to explain why X has a certain property F by saying that Y has property F and X = Y. (It wouldn't be much of an explanation to say that the evening star is bright because the morning star is bright and the evening star is the morning star.) On Block and Stalnaker's approach, the question why such a thing as consciousness exists in this world turns into the question why there is such a thing as pyramidal cell activity. The mystery of consciousness, then, is reduced to the "mystery" of pyramidal cell activity, which doesn't seem like much of a mystery; at least it is not the mystery with which we began. Block and Stalnaker, and like-minded type physicalists, would welcome this result as the hoped-for elimination of the supposed but groundless mystery; these identities would, in their view, put an end to the gratuitous mystery-mongering by the emergentists, Huxley, and the rest. Going back to the issue of reduction vs. reductive explanation, we see that, on Block and Stalnaker's approach, we have reduction but no reductive explanation. This is in contrast with the functional reductive solution to the problem of the gap which gives us both reduction and reductive explanation.

In any case, it would seem that here we are at a standoff between identity reductionists, like Block and Stalnaker, and emergentists. Emergentists may very well want to rule out these identities precisely on the ground that they illegitimatize questions about consciousness that are perfectly intelligible, though unanswerable. This means that we are here in need of an *independent* and *neutral* ground for accepting or rejecting these Kripkean mind-body identities. What would be question-begging is for the identity reductionists to argue that these identities are warranted just because, or at least partly because, they make the emergentists' embarrassing questions about consciousness go away. Similarly, it would be question-begging for the emergentists to reject the identities on the ground that they render their own favorite questions improper and wrongheaded. It is clear, therefore, that Block and Stalnaker's proposals depend crucially on the strength of the ground for embracing identities like (K). If there are compelling scientific or philosophical reasons for accepting the likes of (K), that ought to silence the emergentists.

So what can Block and Stalnaker offer as a warrant for these identities? I think this is the critical question for them and other new identity theorists, like Christopher Hill and Brian McLaughlin. Recall Block and Stalnaker's argument against functional reduction, which goes like this: "Of course, if mental properties are functionally definable, that would be wonderful—it would give us reductive explanation of consciousness and close the explanatory gap. The only trouble is, these functional definitions are just not available." Block and Stalnaker must be able to resist this obvious rejoinder: "Of course, if mental properties can be type-identified with physical/neural properties, that would be wonderful—it would give us reduction and help rid us of the explanatory gap. The only trouble is, these psychoneural identities are just not available." What can Block and Stalnaker, and their type physicalist friends, say in rebuttal? Do they have a positive argument to show that we are indeed entitled to these identities? They claim they do. This will be our next topic.

5

Explanatory Arguments for Type Physicalism and Why They Don't Work

ONE NOTABLE development in the debates over the mind-body problem during the last dozen or so years so is the revival of type physicalism, the view that mental properties and kinds are identical with physical properties and kinds. This was the original form of the mind-body identity theory advanced by Herbert Feigl and J.J.C. Smart in the late 1950s, a position that began losing favor with philosophers by the late 1960s and was abandoned by a large majority of philosophers by the mid-1970s. Much of the current push toward, or back to, type physicalism appears to be a reaction to Joseph Levine's explanatory-gap problem, or what David Chalmers has called the hard problem of consciousness. The central idea is that the explanatory gap between consciousness and the brain could be closed if we could identify states of consciousness with states of the brain. Brian Loar, an early proponent of the new type physicalism, writes:

> It is my view that we can have it both ways. We may take the phenomenological intuition at face value, accepting intro-spective concepts and their conceptual irreducibility, and at the same time take phenomenal qualities to be identical with

physical-functional properties of the sort envisaged by contemporary brain science. As I see it, *there is no persuasive philosophically articulated argument to the contrary.*[1]

Note what Loar says in the last sentence of this paragraph; it is indicative of the attitude common among current type physicalists, and it is reminiscent of Smart's attitude in 1959 when he first proposed the identity theory. Without much exaggeration, it can be characterized as follows: "*I say* that pain is identical with C-fiber stimulation, and *I say* that sensations are identical with brain processes. Refute me if you don't like it!" In his classic paper, "Sensations and Brain Processes," Smart gestures toward a positive argument for his theory based on simplicity considerations, but the obvious emphasis is on the absence of coercive negative arguments; he says "it is the object of this paper to show that there are no philosophical arguments which compel us to be dualists."[2] It is no accident that Smart devotes the bulk of his paper to answering putative objections, all eight of them! This strategy is unsurprising because Smart doesn't think there can be empirical or scientific arguments for or against the identity theory. He writes:

> ... if the issue is between ... some form of materialism on the one hand and epiphenomenalism on the other hand, then the issue is not an empirical one. For there is no conceivable experiment which could decide between materialism and epiphenomenalism.[3]

Here Smart speaks only of "experimental" evidence, but it is clear from the context that he does not believe there could be

1. Brian Loar, "Phenomenal States," reprinted in *The Nature of Consciousness*, ed. Ned Block, Owen Flanagan, and Güven Güzeldere (Cambridge, MA: MIT Press, 1999), p. 598. Originally published in *Philosophical Persepectives* 4 (1990), 81–108. Added emphasis.

2. J.J.C. Smart, "Sensations and Brain Processes," reprinted in *The Nature of Mind*, ed. David M. Rosenthal (New York and Oxford: Oxford University Press, 1991), p. 170. Originally published in *Philosophical Review* 68 (1959): 141–56.

3. "Sensations and Brain Processes," p. 175 (in the Rosenthal volume).

a broadly scientific argument or ground favoring the mind-brain identity hypothesis over epiphenomenalism or other dualist alternatives. Christopher Hill is exactly right when he observes that "instead of giving carefully formulated positive arguments, the materialists of Smart's era relied mainly on sketchy appeals to simplicity and terse complaints about the obscurity and messiness of competing views.[4]

ARE THERE POSITIVE ARGUMENTS FOR TYPE PHYSICALISM?

But what can be said that would give positive support for mind-body identification, something that might persuade someone who has no antecedent physicalist commitments, or perhaps even convert a dualist? What are the positive reasons or grounds for accepting type physicalism? Perhaps, a dualist, too, can refute, or somehow neutralize, all the philosophical objections we can throw at him—at least, to his and his committed friends' satisfaction. Some of the current writers who favor type physicalism focus only on showing that the identification of a sensory quality with a neural/physical property is not conceptually or otherwise incoherent, and therefore that it remains a metaphysical and epistemic possibility. But that is far from showing that psychoneural identification has something positive to recommend it. Fortunately, some recent writers have addressed this issue, coming up with significant proposals for positive grounds for type physicalism. Here I have in mind Christopher Hill, Brian McLaughlin, Ned Block and Robert Stalnaker, all of whom have formulated what I will call explanatory arguments for type physicalism. The argument advanced jointly by Block and Stalnaker differs markedly from

---

4. Christopher S. Hill, *Sensations* (Cambridge: Cambridge University Press, 1991), p. 19.

the argument of the kind formulated by Hill and McLaughlin; in fact, as we will see, the two arguments are at odds with each other. Nevertheless, their central theme is the same: mind-brain identities can play certain critical and indispensable *explanatory* functions, and this confers upon them sufficient warrant for acceptance.[5] Before we go on with an examination of these arguments, let me make some general remarks about possible positive arguments for type physicalism.

Any positive argument for type physicalism must come up with reasons for moving from psychoneural correlations to psychoneural identities—that is, from, say, "pain occurs if and only if C-fiber stimulation occurs" to "pain is identical with C-fiber stimulation." The thesis that there are pervasive psychoneural correlations is widely accepted. But the existence of such correlations is consistent with many dualist theories, like epiphenomenalism, emergentism, and even substance dualism; in fact, it is entailed by some of them. The critical question, therefore, is what grounds there are that make it compelling, or at least reasonable, to upgrade the correlations to identities. As I see it, there are three types of arguments that could be, and have been, advanced on behalf of psychoneural type identities. The first, originally promoted by Smart without much elaboration, is the simplicity argument, to the effect that identifying mental states, including states of consciousness, with neural/physical states of the brain, helps us attain the simplest, most parsimonious worldview. The second is the explanatory approach I have just described.[6] The last is the causal argument, and it is the one I believe works best if anything does.

5. In a book that has just been published, *A Physicalist Manifesto* (Cambridge: Cambridge University Press, 2003), Andrew Melnyk, too, presents an "inference to the best explanation" argument for physicalism (his "realization physicalism").
6. In *Sensations*, Hill recognizes these three arguments for type physicalism; however, he thinks very little of the causal argument, putting his money on the explanatory argument (as we will see).

The canonical form of the argument is very simple and goes like this: Mentality has causal effects in the physical world; however, the physical world is causally closed; therefore, mentality must be part of the physical world, and, specifically, mental states are identical with brain states. David Papineau's argument in his recent book[7] is a good example of this form of the causal argument. Donald Davidson's well-known argument for anomalous monism[8] is another causal argument for physicalism, although the physicalism it endorses is what is known as token physicalism—and a quite weak form of it at that. Of the three arguments in support of type physicalism, I believe the causal argument is the only one that goes some real distance, although not far enough.[9] The explanatory arguments, as I will try to show, are seriously flawed and incapable of generating any real support for type physicalism. As for the simplicity argument, I believe it is difficult to formulate it in a non–question-begging way, though it can provide reassurances to those who are already committed physicalists. What a physicalist may seize upon as the most parsimonious and elegant ontology would be apt to strike the dualist as a hopelessly inadequate scheme which discards, or ignores, the entities that are needed to save the phenomena. A simple and direct appeal to Ockham's razor of the sort Smart makes is unlikely to leave much of an impression on the serious dualist, and it is doubtful that it would sway the uncommitted. For the genuinely uncommitted are uncommitted only because they haven't made up their minds about just what phenomena must be saved in an overall ontology of the world, or, what comes to the same,

7. David Papineau, *Thinking about Consciousness* (Oxford: Oxford University Press, 2002), ch. 1.

8. Donald Davidson, "Mental Events," reprinted in *Essays on Actions and Events* (Oxford and New York: Oxford University Press, 1980); originally published in 1970.

9. As the reader will recognize, the causal argument and its limits are the main topic of this book.

about what entities fall "beyond necessity." Unless and until the protected group of phenomena has been identified, the simplicity argument cannot even be formulated. The reason is that there are no simplicity arguments in a vacuum; they must all take the general form "This scheme should be accepted because it is the simplest one that saves phenomena X, Y, and Z." Obviously, physicalists and nonphysicalists are not likely to agree on what X, Y, Z are.

Hill's and McLaughlin's Explanatory Argument

Hill, who, as we saw, is well aware of the dearth of positive arguments for type physicalism, goes on to say that he is going to remedy this situation by offering an argument based on the explanatory power of type physicalism, referring to it as "the strongest reason for preferring type physicalism"[10] over its competitors. His strategy is to appeal to the so-called principle of inference to the best explanation, first explicitly formulated by Gilbert Harman,[11] and argue that type physicalism, which identifies psychological types with neural/physical types, is the best explanation of the pervasive fact of psychophysical correlations. In his view, this shows "decisively that type physicalism is the *correct* answer to the mind-body problem."[12]

McLaughlin takes a similar approach in his defense of type physicalism for sensory experience.[13] McLaughlin begins by noting that the following claim, affirming the existence of

---

10. *Sensations*, p. 22.

11. Gilbert Harman, "The Inference to the Best Explanation," *Philosophical Review* 74 (1966): 88–95.

12. *Sensations*, p. 24. Emphasis added.

13. Brian P. McLaughlin, "In Defense of New Wave Materialism: A Response to Horgan and Tienson," in *Physicalism and Its Discontents*, ed. Carl Gillett and Barry Loewer (Cambridge: Cambridge University Press, 2001).

lawful correlations between sensory experiences and physical/functional states, is widely accepted:[14]

> *Correlation Thesis.* For every type of sensation state, S, there is a type of physical state P such that it is nomologically necessary that for any organism, x, x is in S if and only if x is in P.

As McLaughlin notes, the Correlation Thesis itself will not suffice as a solution to the mind-body problem, since it is consistent with a host of competing responses to the problem, such as epiphenomenalism, the dual-aspect theory, and emergentism. McLaughlin claims, however, that the doctrine of type physicalism, namely:

> *Type Identity Thesis.* For every type of sensation state, S, there is a type of physical state, P, such that S = P.

offers "*the best explanation* of the correlation thesis."[15] Unlike Hill, McLaughlin does not explicitly advert to the principle of inference to the best explanation; he only appeals to what he calls considerations of "overall coherence and theoretical simplicity."[16] In one respect, though, McLaughlin goes further than Hill: he says that since these psychophysical identities, as "Kripkean" identities, are metaphysically necessary, they can explain the lawlikeness of the psychophysical correlations, in virtue of the fact that metaphysical necessity entails nomological necessity. In any case, the explanatory argument under consideration seems to run on two levels. First, specific psychoneural correlations (for example, the correlation "pain occurs iff C-fiber stimulation occurs") are explained by the corresponding identities (the identity "pain = Cfs"). Second, the general thesis

---

14. McLaughlin, "In Defense of New Wave Materialism," p. 319. I have slightly simplified McLaughlin's formulation; in particular, I have replaced his "physical/functional" with "physical." This should make no difference to the discussion to follow.

15. "In Defense of New Wave Materialism," p. 319.

16. "In Defense of New Wave Materialism," pp. 320, 323.

of psychophysical correlation, that is, McLaughlin's "Correlation Thesis" above, is explained by type physicalism, namely the "Type Identity Thesis." As I take it, each is claimed to be the "best" explanation available for its explanandum.

Hill's and McLaughlin's explanatory arguments prompt a host of questions. Let us begin by noting that inference to the best explanation is standardly thought to be inductive, or "ampliative," inference; this was originally claimed by Harman and it is endorsed by Hill. (McLaughlin, however, must be exempted from the following remarks, since he is silent on this issue and there seems no reason to think that he conceives of his argument as a form of inductive inference.) If inference to the best explanation is inductive inference, we may legitimately raise this question: Is the warrant or justification that the present application of the inference confers on its conclusion, type physicalism, weighty and compelling enough to make it rational for us to accept it *as true*? Even if we were to grant that type physicalism is to be preferred over its rivals, the warrant it enjoys might be far from sufficient for it to merit our "outright" belief or acceptance.[17] And the fact that the *truth* of type physicalism, not just its status as a preferred choice, is what is at issue is clear from Hill's statement of the inference to the best explanation principle:

> If a theory provides a good explanation of a set of facts, and the explanation is better than any explanation provided by a competing theory, there is a good and sufficient reason for believing that the theory is *true*.[18]

17. "Outright belief" in something like Timothy Williamson's sense, in his *Knowledge and Its Limits* (Oxford: Oxford University Press, 2000), p. 99. Outright beliefs are beliefs whose contents the believer is prepared to use as premises in practical inference.

18. *Sensations*, p. 22. Added emphasis. McLaughlin, however, does not make an explicit claim of truth on behalf of type physicalism, although it seems clear that he thinks that the explanatory argument lends type physicalism sufficient warrant for our acceptance.

And, as noted earlier, Hill takes his explanatory argument to "show decisively that type materialism is the correct answer to the mind-body problem."[19] But what if the explanation offered by type physicalism for psychophysical correlations is only marginally better than those offered by its competitors?

There are other serious questions to think about concerning this application of inference to the best explanation. Given that type physicalism is to be compared with its rivals in point of explanatory power, why are these theories tested *only* in respect of how well they explain psychophysical correlations? Inductive reasoning, whose aim is to reach a conclusion that we should believe as true, or be prepared to use as a guide to action, must respect the principle of *total evidence*, and in the present case this means that the data, or evidence, to be explained must be all the data relevant to the issue on hand.[20] It may not be clear exactly what these data are in the present case, but surely it is arbitrary to consider only the fact of psychophysical correlations. Dualists will say that among the relevant data are such things as the presumptive authoritativeness and privacy of first-person access to one's own mental states, the persistence condition of persons, the multiple physical realizability of mental properties, the possibility of qualia inversions, the possibility of "zombies," and the like. These are all contested and disputed issues; however, like it or not, dealing with them *is* the mind-body problem.[21] What we should not do, it seems to me, is to pick the fact of psychoneural correlations alone as the

19. *Sensations*, p. 24.

20. In this sense, Hill's statement of the rule of inference to the best explanation quoted above is incomplete in referring to a theory giving the best explanation of "a set of facts." Which set of facts? Clearly, reference should be made to something like "all the facts in the domain."

21. In his further defense of type physicalism in *Sensations*, Hill addresses many of these issues, often in a sensitive and persuasive way. In doing this, though, Hill appears to be conceding that his explanatory argument by itself could not be a decisive ground for type physicalism.

explanandum, and argue that since type physicalism offers the best explanation of this datum, it must be the overall winner—and, moreover, it must be *true!* It is possible that type physicalism gives the best overall account of all these facts, but that must be shown, and that would go far beyond the kind of explanatory argument under consideration.

One last general point about the explanatory argument: part of what lends plausibility to the talk of inference to the best explanation in empirical science is the fact that putting competing theories to test on the basis of how well they explain the data is an ongoing, in-principle never-ending, affair. When further data are in, the rankings of the theories in terms of their explanatory power may very well change. Or what comes to the same thing: we subject the theories to further test by deriving new predictions from them. That is typical of—some will say, constitutive of—what goes on in the "inductive" sciences. But this feature seems entirely lacking in the application of the explanatory test to the competing mind-body theories. Here, as the advocates of the explanatory argument see it, it seems like an open-and-shut affair. There seems no possible further evidence, or data, to determine whether the current winner of the explanatory battle will continue to reign; and it is difficult to conceive what *further* evidence might be uncovered in the future that might favor, say, epiphenomenalism over type physicalism, or the double-aspect theory over emergentism. Inference to the best explanation has been advertised as inductive inference, but it is prima facie implausible that an inductive rule could determine the fate of these rival theories of the mind—or philosophical theories in general. One final point: this obviously is not a place to raise general questions about the status of the rule of inference to the best explanation, but we should keep in mind the fact that explanation is a plastic and fragile notion; some will say that what counts as an explanation is a highly context-sensitive (if not outright relative or subjective) and pragmatic affair, and we should be cautious, if not suspicious, about any inference rule that essentially rests on considerations of explanation.[22]

Do Psychoneural Identities Explain Psychoneural Correlations?

Let us now turn to a more basic, and absolutely central, question: Do identities explain correlations, as claimed by Hill and McLaughlin? Does the identity "pain = C-fiber stimulation" really *explain* the correlation "pain occurs ↔ Cfs occurs" (I am using "↔" to mean "if and only if"), and if so, how does it do it? What does the explanation look like? And what kind of explanation is it? These questions are of critical importance to the explanatory argument. For if specific psychoneural identities do not explain the corresponding correlations, there is no hope that type physicalism (McLaughlin's "Type Identity Thesis") will explain the general psychoneural correlation thesis (McLaughlin's "Correlation Thesis").

Consider then the following argument:

(α)   (K) Pain = C-fiber stimulation.
       Therefore, (C) Pain occurs ↔ Cfs occurs.

As I take it, Hill and McLaughlin will make the following claims: first, (K) logically implies the correlation (C); second, (K) thereby explains (C)—that is, (α) is an explanatory argument. These claims assume that identities, in particular necessary Kripkean identities, can generate explanations in their own right. Is this correct?

---

22. It seems to me that in most cases where inference to the best explanation is invoked, all that "explanation" amounts to is logical implication or deduction, and logical deducibility seems the only substantive and robust core of the talk of explanation. For a general discussion and critique of inference to the best explanation, see Bas van Fraassen, *Laws and Symmetry* (Oxford: Oxford University Press, 1989).

Suppose someone claims that he has an explanation of why Cicero is wise, and proceeds to offer the following argument as his explanation:

(β) Tully is wise.
     Tully = Cicero.
     Therefore, Cicero is wise.

If anyone should offer this as an explanation of why Cicero is wise, we surely would not take it seriously. Compare this argument with the following:

This steel rod is being heated.
Metals expand when heated.
Therefore, this rod is expanding.

Unlike the law "Metals expand when heated" involved in this plainly explanatory argument, the identity "Tully = Cicero" in (β) seems to do no explanatory work. If it does anything to move the inference along, it is by allowing us to *rewrite* the premise "Tully is wise" as "Cicero is wise," by putting equals for equals (that is, via the substitutivity of identities). The fact represented by the first premise "Tully is wise" is the very same fact as the fact represented by the conclusion "Cicero is wise"; in moving from premise to conclusion, the same fact is redescribed. There is no movement here from one fact to another, something that surely must happen in a genuine explanatory argument. Identities seem best taken as mere rewrite rules in inferential contexts; they generate no explanatory connections between the explanandum and the phenomena invoked in the explanans; they seem not to have explanatory efficacy of their own.[23]

23. Here I am speaking only of necessary identities with rigid designators, not contingent identities like "Margaret Okayo was the women's winner of the 2003 New York Marathon" and "Jerry is the fastest talker among philosophers," which seem eminently explainable.

These remarks are in accord with what Block and Stalnaker say about the role of identities in explanations. In their argument against the view that a reductive explanation of a phenomenon (say, consciousness) requires an a priori conceptual connection between the phenomenon and the base phenomenon that explains it, they write:[24]

> All we reject is the a priori, purely conceptual status attributed to the bridge principles connecting the ordinary description of the phenomenon to be explained with its description in the language of science. What is actually deduced in such an explanation is a description wholly within the language of science of the phenomenon to be explained. For this to answer the original explanatory question, posed in so-called folk vocabulary, all we need to add is the claim that the phenomenon described in scientific language is the same ordinary phenomenon described in a different way.

Suppose someone asks, in "folk vocabulary", "Why did Jones lose consciousness at time t?" The following will serve as an explanation:

> Jones was given an injection of sodium pentothal shortly before t.
> Administration of sodium pentothal to a patient causes pyramidal cell activity to cease.
> Therefore, pyramidal cell activity ceased in Jones at t.
> Consciousness = pyramidal cell activity.
> Therefore, Jones lost consciousness at t.

On Block and Stalnaker's view, explanatory activity is over at the third line. What the Kripkean identity, "consciousness = pyramidal cell activity," does is to enable us to rewrite the

---

24. Ned Block and Robert Stalnaker, "Conceptual Analysis, Dualism, and the Explanatory Gap," *Philosophical Review* 108 (1999): 1–46. The quotation is from pp. 8–9.

explanandum statement, redescribing in folk vocabulary the phenomenon that has already been explained. This allows us to claim that we have explained why Jones lost consciousness at t. That is, identities do not play a role in generating explanations; they only allow us to redescribe facts. I believe this is a plausible view.

Moreover, the kind of "explanation" represented by (α) above seems entirely unlike scientific explanations of correlations. In science there seem to be two principal ways of explaining correlations: first, correlations are sometimes explained by invoking a single lower-level process or structure underlying the correlated phenomena; second, the explanation may proceed by showing the correlated phenomena to be collateral effects of a common cause. For example, the correlation between thermal and electrical conductivity is explained by the fact that both types of conduction involve the movement of free electrons through the lattice structure of metals. And we may explain the correlations between tidal movements and the phases of the moon by showing both to be causal effects of the relative positions of the earth and the moon in relation to the sun. Explanations of these kinds are very familiar both in everyday life and in the sciences;[25] they are substantive explanations subject to further tests and possible falsifications. And they contrast sharply with the seemingly empty explanations of the kind offered in (α). In any case, it is quite obvious that scientists will not in general attempt to explain correlations by identifying the correlated properties—for example, by identifying thermal and electrical conductivity, or high temperatures and the glowing of an iron bar.

An explanation, when it is deductive, is best thought of as a derivation, not just a display of the premises and conclusion as

---

25. If we take the correlations to be laws, there is a general way of explaining laws, namely by deriving them from more basic laws.

in (α). To gain a real explanatory insight, we must see how the conclusion can be derived, step by step, from the explanatory premises. That is, an explanation is a proof, not just a listing of the explanatory premises and explanandum. How might we derive the explanatory conclusion "pain occurs ↔ Cfs occurs" from the identity "pain = Cfs"? To my knowledge, there is no rule in logic that says "From 'X = Y,' infer 'X occurs ↔ Y occurs.'" Rather, first-order logic standardly offers the following two rules involving identity:[26]

Axiom schema: X = X.
Rule of substitution: From "...X...." and "X = Y," infer "...Y....".

Given this, the only way I see how a derivation of a correlation from an identity might go is like this:

(γ)   Pain occurs ↔ pain occurs.
      Pain = Cfs.
      Therefore, pain occurs ↔ Cfs occurs.

The first line is an instance of the truth-functional tautology "p ↔ p," and the identity of the second line allows us to rewrite it in accordance with the rule of substitution, by putting "Cfs" for the second occurrence of "pain" in the first line. (Obviously, we could have begun with the tautology "Cfs occurs ↔ Cfs occurs" as the initial premise.)

Does the derivation, (γ), look to you like an explanation of a correlation in terms of an identity? Does it look to you like any kind of explanation? It surely does not to me. The sole explanatory premise is the tautologous "pain occurs ↔ pain occurs," an instance of a factually empty logical truth. The purported explanandum is simply a rewrite of this plainest of

26. See, e.g., Elliott Mendelson, *Introduction to Mathematical Logic* (Princeton: D. Van Nostrand, 1964), p. 75.

all tautologies, and as such it reports no new fact beyond the "fact" reported by "pain occurs ↔ pain occurs." This derivation seems no more explanatory than the derivation, (β), of "Cicero is wise" from "Tully is wise." It is a far cry from genuine, factually substantial and empirically falsifiable, explanations of correlations found in the sciences.

We don't have to say identities have absolutely no role in explanatory contexts. What identities can do is to help *defend* or *justify* explanatory claims. Schematically this works as follows: "We have explained why X is F, because X = Y and we have an explanation of why Y is F." Consider: "We have explained why when water freezes its volume increases, because water = H_2O, and our physical theory explains why when a quantity of H_2O molecules turns into a solid its volume increases." Further, if we take sentences or statements as explananda, we can say that identities enlarge the domain of our explanations. I believe the view advocated here assigns a simple but important role to identities in explanation. It can explain the vaunted additional explanatory power sometimes assigned to scientific identities like "water = H_2O," "light = electromagnetic radiation," "genes = DNA molecules," and the rest, in a simple and satisfying way, without regarding identities themselves as generating new explanations of facts and regularities.

To return to the issue of identities and correlations, it has been argued plausibly that the whole point of identities is that they enable us to *transcend* correlations, not explain them. Recall what Smart said about identities versus correlations in his 1959 paper:

> That [the states of consciousness like visual, auditory, and tactual sensations, and aches and pains] are *correlated* with brain processes does not help, for to say that they are *correlated* is to say that they are something "over and above." You cannot correlate something with itself. You can correlate footprints with burglars, but not Bill Sikes the burglar with Bill Sikes the

burglar. So sensations, states of consciousness, do seem to be the one sort of thing left outside the physical picture, and for various reasons I just cannot believe that this can be so.[27]

For Smart, then, identities and correlations exclude each other. We ascend to psychoneural identities in order to discard and transcend psychoneural correlations. The identity "pain = Cfs" enables us to do away with the correlation "pain occurs ↔ Cfs occurs." And as physicalists we must rid ourselves of this correlation because qua correlation it countenances pains as something "over and above" Cfs. Herbert Feigl, another original type physicalist, took a similar line: the correlation "pain occurs ↔ Cfs occurs" is a "nomological dangler" which the identity "pain = Cfs" enables us to get rid of.[28] On this approach, psychoneural identities get their warrant precisely from the fact that they eliminate psychoneural correlations or "dangling" laws, not from the supposed explanations they provide for them.

To counter Smart's remarks, one might say that there is an interpretation of the correlation that makes it compatible with the identity, and it is this: Given "pain = Cfs," all that the correlation "pain occurs ↔ Cfs occurs" says is what the harmless tautologies "pain occurs ↔ pain occurs" and "Cfs occurs ↔ Cfs occurs" say, and neither of these needs to be taken to imply that pains are "over and above" Cfs. But this can scarcely be considered a defense of the line McLaughlin and Hill are taking about the explanation of correlations by identities. As derived à la (γ), "pain occurs ↔ Cfs occurs" says no more than "pain occurs ↔ pain occurs" or "Cfs occurs ↔ Cfs occurs," and this means that we have in effect lost our original explanandum; that is, the correlation, which we took to be empirical and significant (remember that McLaughlin considers it a law) has turned into an

---

27. Smart, "Sensations and Brain Processes," in Rosenthal, *The Nature of Mind*, p. 169. Emphasis in the original.

28. Herbert Feigl, "The 'Mental' and the 'Physical,' " *Minnesota Studies in the Philosophy of Science*, vol. 2 (Minneapolis: University of Minnesota Press, 1958.)

instance of "p ↔ p," leaving nothing of significance to be explained. So Smart's perspective on this could be put this way: If we have the identity "pain = Cfs" in hand, it is not the case that we can explain the correlation "pain ↔ Cfs" with the identity; rather, the identity shows that there is here nothing to be explained. If anyone should ask "Why is it the case that pains correlate with Cfs?", we should reply that pains are Cfs, and that pain no more correlates with Cfs than pain correlates with pain. Talk of correlation here makes no better sense than in the case of water and H_2O, or light and electromagnetic radiation. That seems to me like the right response. As for the explanatory gap between pain and Cfs, the identity "pain = Cfs" shows that the supposed gap is not there—it never was. Since there is one thing here, not two, there is no gap to close or bridge.

What I have been saying is in accord with Block and Stalnaker's views on identities vis-à-vis correlations. They, too, argue for type physicalism on explanatory grounds, but their approach is quite different from—actually, opposed to—McLaughlin's and Hill's. Psychoneural identities help us with explanations, on their view, but not as explanations of the associated correlations. Here is what they say:

> If we believe that heat is correlated with but not identical to molecular kinetic energy, we should regard as legitimate the question of why the correlation exists and what its mechanism is. But once we realize that heat *is* molecular kinetic energy, questions like this will be seen as wrongheaded.[29]

As we saw, emergentists have claimed that explanatory questions like "Why does pain correlate with Cfs?", "Why doesn't pain correlate with Aδ-fiber stimulation?", "Why doesn't itch correlate with Cfs?", and "Why does any conscious experience correlate with Cfs?" could not in principle be answered, and that, for this reason, the phenomena of emergence must be accepted and

29. Block and Stalnaker, "Conceptual Analysis, Dualism, and the Explanatory Gap," p. 24.

physicalism rejected. Block and Stalnaker are saying that one important philosophical function of an identity like "pain = Cfs" is to show these requests for explanation to be "wrong-headed" and improper. Why? Because, as was just noted, given the identity, the correlation vanishes, leaving nothing to be explained. The identity "pain = Cfs" rescinds the correlation, and thereby voids the presupposition of the question "Why does pain correlate with Cfs, not with another neural state?" Since this why-question has a false presupposition, it has no correct answer.[30] These explanatory why-questions can be dealt with—by showing that they are, as Block and Stalnaker put it, "wrong-headed," not by providing them with answers. This reading of Block and Stalnaker, therefore, puts them on Smart and Feigl's side, with Hill and McLaughlin on the opposite side.

BLOCK AND STALNAKER'S EXPLANATORY ARGUMENT

As we saw, Block and Stalnaker's approach to the explanatory gap is via the type identification of sensory states with neural/physical states. If we can identify pain with Cfs, there can be no gap between the two; only when we allow them to be diverse, the issue of an explanatory gap can arise. The closing of the gap via an identity, they claim, makes potentially embarrassing explanatory questions go away. These questions, and the gap, will remain to haunt us if we refuse to acknowledge the identity of pain with Cfs.[31]

30. On why-questions, see Sylvain Bromberger, "Why-Questions," in *Mind and Cosmos*, ed. Robert Colodny (Pittsburgh: Pittsburgh University Press, 1966).

31. For this to hold, Block and Stalnaker have to argue for one more claim, namely that these identities are not themselves subject to explanatory challenges—that is, they are not the sort of thing that can be, or need to be, explained. As long as it makes sense to ask "Why is pain identical with Cfs, not with Aδ-fiber stimulation?" and similar questions, the explanatory gap will re-open. Block and Stalnaker understandably take the view that identities are not explainable ("Conceptual Analysis, Dualism, and the Explanatory Gap," p. 24).

We can grant all this—if we had "pain = Cfs" and other such psychoneural identities, that would indeed be dandy! We could then rid ourselves of the explanatory gap and dismiss as wrongheaded all those explanatory demands that inspired a whole philosophical movement, emergentism, with its dubious commitment to "downward causation." We can agree with Block and Stalnaker that these psychoneural identities would be highly desirable things to have. But where do we get them? What are the grounds for thinking they are true? What is the basis of our entitlement to these identities? Block and Stalnaker take this question seriously and try to provide an answer. I think their answer, like the argument of Hill and McLaughlin, is seriously flawed, and I will try to show you why.

Block and Stalnaker take psychoneural identities like "pain = Cfs" and "consciousness = pyramidal cell activity" (an example they take out of the research by Francis Crick and Christof Koch[32]) as belonging to a familiar class of identities, which Hilary Putnam once called "theoretical identifications,"[33] like the following:

Water = H_2O.
Heat = molecular kinetic energy.
Light = electromagnetic radiation.

We have been calling these "Kripkean" identities, necessary a posteriori identity statements that tell us what the "real nature" of some object or phenomenon is. Block and Stalnaker's crucial claim is that psychoneural identities like "pain = Cfs" can be justified, or epistemically grounded, in exactly the same

32. For a popular presentation of this work, see Francis Crick, *The Astonishing Hypothesis* (New York: Scribner, 1994).
33. Hilary Putnam, "Minds and Machines," in *Mind, Language, and Reality* (Cambridge: Cambridge University Press, 1975); first published in 1960.

way these familiar scientific identities are justified and grounded.

Let us first see how, according to Block and Stalnaker, these scientific identities are justified—from what they derive their warrant. Here is what they say:

> Why do we suppose that heat = molecular kinetic energy? Consider the explanation given above of why heating water makes it boil. Suppose that heat = molecular kinetic energy, pressure = molecular momentum transfer, and boiling = a certain kind of molecular motion. . . . Then we have an account of how heating water produces boiling. If we were to accept mere correlations instead of identities, we would only have an account of how something correlated with heating causes something correlated with boiling. . . . Identities allow a transfer of explanatory and causal force not allowed by mere correlations. Assuming that heat = mke, that pressure = molecular momentum transfer, etc. allows us to explain facts that we could not otherwise explain. Thus, we are justified by *the principle of inference to the best explanation* in inferring that these identities are true.[34]

In this paragraph, Block and Stalnaker build an apparently plausible case for the identities, heat with mke and pressure with molecular momentum transfer, on explanatory grounds. Notice especially their explicit appeal to the principle of inference to the best explanation: acceptance of these identities is sufficiently justified because they enable explanations that mere correlations could not yield. In fact, on Block and Stalnaker's view, identities have a dual explanatory role: on one hand, they enable certain explanations that we want to have, and on the other, as we have seen, they "disable," as we might say, certain explanatory questions that we are better off not

---

34. Block and Stalnaker, "Conceptual Analysis, Dualism, and the Explanatory Gap," pp. 23–24. Emphasis added.

having to face, like "Why is there water where and only where there is H_2O?"

What then of psychoneural identities? Block and Stalnaker write:

> Suppose that there is an a posteriori truth of the form consciousness = brain state B. Recall the suggestion by Crick and Koch, mentioned earlier, that consciousness is pyramidal cell activity. . . .
>
> Without the help of conceptual analysis, how might such an identity claim be justified? By using the kinds of methodological considerations sketched in our discussion of simplicity above—*the same kinds of considerations that are used to justify water = H_2O.*[35]

This proposal is bold and surprising—and more than a little incredible! For Block and Stalnaker are saying in effect that the mind-body problem is a scientific research problem on the order of the discovery that water = H_2O and that heat = molecular kinetic energy. Not that these and other similar scientific discoveries were easy or entirely straightforward, or that scientific methodology is irrelevant to philosophical debates. Rather, the point is that it is difficult to believe that a problem that has long vexed so many great minds in western philosophy, including some of the finest scientists, dividing them into a host of warring camps, should turn out to be something that could have been solved the same way that scientists determined the molecular structure of water. As we saw earlier, not even Smart, perhaps the most sanguine of the contemporary materialists, thought that the choice between type physicalism and dualism was a matter to be decided by science.

Our task here, however, is to analyze and evaluate the merits of Block and Stalnaker's argument. Let us first see what they

---

35. Block and Stalnaker, "Conceptual Analysis, Dualism, and the Explanatory Gap," p. 29. Emphasis added.

are saying about the case of boiling water. Consider the two hypotheses below, (Corr) and (Id):

> (Corr) Water correlates with H_2O; heating water correlates with the increase of mke of the H_2O molecules; the boiling of water correlates with molecular activity M of the H_2O molecules.

> (Id) Water = H_2O; heating water = increasing mke of the H_2O molecules; the boiling of water = molecular activity M of the H_2O molecules.

We have a well-confirmed and well-understood physical theory that explains in detail the process whereby increasing mke of H_2O molecules causes molecular activity M. So (Id) yields the following derivation:

> (δ) P (physical theory)
> Increasing mke of H_2O causes molecular activity M.
> (Id)
> Therefore, heating water causes water to boil.

Line 2 is derived from physical theory P, and P explains it. Using (Id) and the rule of substitution, we then derive the conclusion, and we can now claim that we have an explanation of why heating water causes it to boil. We can say, with Block and Stalnaker, that the identities of (Id) allow a "transfer" of explanatory and causal force. Compare this with the situation in which we would find ourselves if we were to accept (Corr) but not (Id). (Corr) would only sanction the following derivation:

> (ε) P (physical theory)
> Increasing mke of H_2O causes molecular activity M.
> (Corr)
> Therefore, heating water is correlated with a phenomenon which causes the phenomenon with which boiling is correlated.

Here there is no explanation of why heating water causes it to boil. (Corr) does not enable the explanatory force of physical theory P to reach the phenomenon given in folk language. But this is exactly what (Id) can accomplish. Since (Id) makes it possible for us to explain a fact—and numerous other facts— that we formerly were unable to explain, we are justified, Block and Stalnaker tell us, by the principle of inference to the best explanation, in concluding that these identities are true.

And Block and Stalnaker are saying that the same pattern of reasoning justifies a transition from psychoneural correlations to psychoneural identities. Suppose our neurophysiology explains why neural state N_1 causes neural state N_2. Moreover, we find that N_1 correlates with pain and that N_2 correlates with a sense of distress. If we stop short of identifying pain with N_1 and distress with N_2, we can only explain why pain correlates with a phenomenon that causes the phenomenon with which a sense of distress is correlated. Only by going to the identities "pain = N_1" and "sense of distress = N_2" can we bring our neurophysiology to bear on the situation and explain why pain causes a feeling of distress. This gives us the following explanatory derivation:

(θ) Neurophysiology
Neural state N_1 causes neural state N_2.
Pain = N_1.
Sense of distress = N_2.
Therefore, pain causes a sense of distress.

Again, Block and Stalnaker would urge us to accept the psychoneural identities "pain = N_1" and "distress = N_2" as true on the ground that these enable us to explain, via neurophysiology, a fact that we would otherwise not be able to explain. Again, the principle of inference to the best explanation would be cited to justify the move from correlations to identities.

That is Block and Stalnaker's argument for psychoneural identities, or type physicalism. So what should we think of this argument? I believe it misfires—I believe this can be shown, in a kind of ad hominem way, using their own remarks on the role of identities in explanation. (My argument is not really ad hominem, because I have endorsed a view of the role of identities very similar to theirs.) Remember an earlier quotation from Block and Stalnaker on this issue, which we used in our discussion of McLaughlin's and Hill—I will restate part of it for ease of reference:

> What is actually deduced in such an explanation is a description wholly within the language of science of the phenomenon to be explained. For this to answer the original explanatory question, posed in so-called folk vocabulary, all we need to add is the claim that the phenomenon described in scientific language is the same ordinary phenomenon described in a different way.[36]

According to Block and Stalnaker, therefore, the explanatory activity, in derivation (θ), is over and done with at the second line, when we have derived "N_1 causes N_2" from neurophysiology, and the only role the identities play is to enable us to restate the phenomenon that has already been explained, the last line of the derivation being this restatement in the "folk" vocabulary. That is to say, the identities "pain = N_1" and "sense of distress = N_2" serve only as *rewrite rules*, and they are not implicated in the explanatory activity. All the explaining represented in the derivation occurs within neurophysiology, and when we derive the second line from neurophysiological theory, we are doing some genuine explaining. And that is the only explaining involved here. The identities kick in only after the explaining is finished. True, these identities do have a role in the derivation of "Pain causes distress," but this is not an explanatory derivation; rather, it is a derivation in which we put

---

36. Block and Stalnaker, "Conceptual Analysis, Dualism, and the Explanatory Gap," pp. 8–9.

"equals for equals," and thereby redescribe in folk vocabulary a phenomenon that has already been explained. That is Block and Stalnaker's own view on the role of identities in explanations, and I believe it is the correct view.

We have to conclude then that Block and Stalnaker's appeal to the principle of inference to the best explanation is misplaced. The identities they hope to validate are simply not implicated in explanations of the sorts Block and Stalnaker have in mind and cannot be the beneficiaries of inference to the best explanation. And, with the McLaughlin-Hill explanatory argument already ruled out, it is difficult to imagine any explanatory roles for identities that would make them eligible for the application of the principle of inference to the best explanation. As we argued, identities do not seem capable of generating explanations on their own; the best they can do is to "transfer" explanations that have already been completed—not from one phenomenon to another phenomenon, but from one *description* of a phenomenon to *another description* of the same phenomenon.

ANOTHER WAY OF LOOKING
AT THE TWO EXPLANATORY ARGUMENTS

The two arguments we have considered, one by McLaughlin and Hill and one by Block and Stalnaker, fail as explanatory arguments, but that does not mean that they fail to make a point or that they have nothing to teach us. I believe that the McLaughlin-Hill argument can be viewed as a simplicity argument, and that the Block-Stalnaker argument can be seen as a causal argument of the kind we are familiar with from elsewhere. I will briefly explain.

In his presentation, McLaughlin puts the explanatory argument in a suggestive way:

> [The Type Identity Thesis] implies the Correlation Thesis. . . . We maintain, *on grounds of overall coherence and theoretical simplicity*, that the explanation of the Correlation Thesis that the Type Identity Thesis offers is superior to the explanations offered by other theories of mind.[37]

I think the "explanation" McLaughlin speaks of here could be taken—and this may well be the way he takes it—to be a philosophical explanation, or philosophical theory-building, rather than a garden-variety scientific explanation to which something like the rule of inference to the best explanation might apply. The fact that McLaughlin, unlike the other philosophers we are considering here, does not explicitly appeal to inference to the best explanation is relevant here. For this reason I believe it is not implausible to take McLaughlin to be arguing that, of all possible stances on the mind-body problem, type physicalism delivers the overall most coherent and simplest ontology.

As for the explanatory argument of Block and Stalnaker, I believe it is perhaps best construed as a form of the familiar causal argument for mind-body reductionism. Consider argument (θ) above. Block and Stalnaker take it to answer this question: How can we explain the fact that pain causes distress? But let us put the question a little differently, without mentioning explanation: How can we show that there is here a causal relation between one mental event and another? How is it possible that pain causes distress? This is the problem of mental causation—or one form of it. The answer: If we can reductively identify pain with N_1 and distress with N_2, we will be

---

37. McLaughlin, "In Defense of New Wave Materialsim," pp. 319–20. Emphasis added.

able to see how pain causes distress, since we have from neuro-physiology a detailed story about how N_1 causes N_2. I am suggesting this as a way of understanding what the inference (θ) above shows. Viewed this way, (θ) is a straightforward causal argument for reductionism, or type physicalism: If mental kinds are identical with physical kinds, that will vindicate mental causation.

But it is important to see that this is not at all a conclusive argument for type physicalism—for two reasons. First, even if we assume that mental causation is real, we would have to show that type identities are the *only* way of showing mental causation to be possible. It may be true—I think it is true—that type physicalism will vindicate mental causation, but it may not be the only position on the mind-body problem that can do this. In my view, functional reduction of the sort I have discussed, which, unlike Block and Stalnaker's type physical-ism, is immune to the notorious multiple realization argu-ment, can also ground mental causation. Second, even if we are entitled to the conditional "Mental causation is possible only if some form of reductionism holds," we cannot infer that reductionism is true. For we should not a priori rule out epiphenomenalism and other noncausal views of the mind. Reductionism must be earned—and mental causation, too, must be earned—by showing that mental properties are in-deed reducible, in a relevant sense, to physical/biological properties. And this requires independent arguments and evi-dence. Mental causation is a presumptive desideratum, and it may be very high on our wish list. But our wish to save mental causation, however sincere and righteous, cannot by itself make reductionism true.

6

Physicalism, or Something Near Enough

As REFLECTIVE and self-aware creatures, we want to know what kind of being we are, what our nature is. We also want to know how we fit into the world we live in, what our place is in this world. But what kind of place is this world, to begin with? For detailed knowledge of the world, we must defer to the deliverances of the sciences. Only science can tell us about the origin of life on earth, the causes and cures of cancer, the depletion of the ozone layer, and the like. On the overall shape and makeup of the world in essential outlines, we must depend on what physics, our fundamental science, tells us. I believe that the broad basic features of the world as described by modern physics, what is intelligible and is of interest to those of us who are not science specialists, has been relatively stable through the flux of changing physical theories, and this is what forms the background of the debates on the mind-body problem.

A philosophical worldview that has been inspired and fostered by an appreciation of the foundational position of physics among the sciences is physicalism. It has shaped much of the philosophical discussion of the mind-body problem through the twentieth century, at least in the analytic tradition, and is likely to continue to do so in the foreseeable future. The core of contemporary physicalism is the idea that all things that exist in this world are bits of matter and structures aggregated out of bits of matter, all behaving in accordance with laws of physics, and that any phenomenon of the world can be physically explained if it can be explained at all. When physicalism is accepted as a basic framework, the foremost metaphysical question about the mind is where in the physical world our minds and mentality fit—indeed, whether minds have a place in a physical world at all. In this chapter, I want to discuss just where we are with the physicalist program, in order to see to what extent physicalism's hopes and promises have been, or are likely to be, realized or frustrated—that is, how much, or what kind of, physicalism we can have. As we will see, the efforts do not succeed entirely, but I will claim that they succeed *nearly enough*. But first we need to review just where we are with the claims and arguments so far advanced in this book.

TAKING STOCK

The most fundamental tenet of physicalism concerns the ontology of the world. It claims that the content of the world is wholly exhausted by matter. Material things are all the things that there are; there is nothing inside the spacetime world that isn't material, and of course there is nothing outside it either. The spacetime world is the whole world, and material things, bits of matter and complex structures made up of bits of matter, are its only inhabitants. This doctrine is sometimes called "ontological physicalism."

But why should we accept ontological physicalism? Why can't there be things other than material things? In an earlier chapter a causal argument was mounted against Cartesian mental substances, minds conceived as concrete immaterial things outside physical space in causal interaction with material things located within physical space. We saw that if minds were such mental substances, they could not possibly causally influence, or be influenced by, material things, and further, they could not causally interact with one another either. That is to say, immaterial nonspatial minds would be totally causally impotent, and this renders them explanatorily irrelevant and useless. Moreover, such a radically noncausal view of minds makes it difficult to understand how we could even come to know that there are minds. Our considerations do not show that causal relations cannot hold within a single mental substance (even Leibniz, famous for disallowing causation between monads, allowed it within a single monad, or so I understand). However, what has been shown, I believe, is sufficient to defeat any rationale for substance dualism. Causality requires a domain with a space-like structure—that is, a "space" within which objects and events can be identified by their "locations"—and, as far as we know, the domain of physical objects is the only domain with a structure of that kind. If this is right, we have a causal argument for monistic physicalist ontology.

Although substance dualism has not been taken as a serious option in mainstream philosophy of mind since the early twentieth century, a general dualist perspective has shown itself to possess a surprisingly tenacious capacity for survival. The dualism of mental and physical properties, in various forms, has dominated the field during the second half of the last century, and continues to hold the allegiance of a majority of philosophers, although it is fair to say that what Ned Block has aptly called "antireductionist consensus," which was firmly in place by the mid-1970s, is no longer what it used to be. I believe the persistence of dualism points to what strikes me as a deeply entrenched, almost instinctive, aversion that most of us feel toward reductionist physicalism. Most of us would like to believe, it seems, that although we are wholly composed of bits of matter, we are extraordinarily complex physical systems with properties, capacities, and functions that are not merely physical or reducible to the merely physical. We are apt to feel that reductive physicalism, according to which thoughts and feelings are mere molecular movements, cannot do justice to the special and distinctive position that we occupy in the natural order, and that a reductionist physicalist is in self-denial, a denial of his own distinctive and unique nature. An idea like this is found not only in those wedded to a traditional, often religiously inspired, conception of ourselves as persons; it also seems to be the driving force behind the widely shared view that the special sciences, especially those concerning humans, like psychology, cognitive science, and economics, are autonomous and irreducible to the physical and biological sciences. Current antireductionism as it concerns the special sciences seems almost like a replay of the influential doctrine in late nineteenth-century Europe that posited a fundamental difference between the *Naturwissenschaften* and the *Geisteswissenschaften*—that is, between the natural sciences and the humane sciences.[1] In any case, the long reign of nonreductive physicalism is a testimony to its appeal as a thesis about the nature of the special sciences as well as a position on the mind-body problem. It promises to safeguard both the autonomy of the special sciences and our specialness as cognizers and agents. But philosophical positions cannot live on hopes and messages alone: they have to deliver the goods as advertised.

As it has turned out, nonreductive materialism could not deliver on mental causation—any better than Cartesian dualism could. It could not explain, on its own terms, how mental phenomena, like belief, desire, feeling, and sensation, could causally affect the course of events in the physical world. Mind-to-body causation is fundamental if our mentality is to make a difference to what goes on in the world. If I want to have the slightest causal influence on anything outside me—to change a light bulb or start a war—I must first move my

1. For a helpful survey of the debate, see Georg von Wright, *Explanation and Understanding* (Ithaca, NY: Cornell University Press, 1971), ch. 1.

limbs or other parts of my body; somehow, my beliefs and desires must cause the muscles in my arms and legs to contract, or cause my vocal cords to vibrate. Mental causation is fundamental to our conception of mentality, and to our view of ourselves as agents and cognizers; any theory of mind that is not able to accommodate mental causation must be considered inadequate, or at best incomplete.

So how can a mental phenomenon, say, my desire for a drink of water, manage to cause my legs to move so as to transport my entire body to the kitchen? Earlier we have discussed in considerable detail an argument, the "supervenience" or "exclusion" argument, whose conclusion is that causally efficacious mental phenomena must be reducible to physical ones, and, more broadly, that, given the closed character of the physical domain, any phenomenon that is causally linked with a physical phenomenon must itself be a physical phenomenon. If mental phenomena are neural processes in the brain, there will be no special mystery about mental causation; I believe we already know the neurophysiology involved well enough—how neural excitations in the motor cortex send electrochemical signals down through the efferent nerve channels to the appropriate muscles, causing them to contract, which in turn causes the limbs to move. According to property dualism, however, mental phenomena are distinct from neural phenomena, and it becomes a prima facie mystery by what mechanisms, or through what intervening links, these supposedly nonphysical phenomena can cause the muscles to contract. At least, this much seems undeniable: If my desire is to cause my legs to move, it must somehow make use of, or ride piggyback on, the causal chain from my motor cortex to the leg muscles. It just is not possible to believe that my desire might be able to act on my legs directly, through some form of telekinesis, or that there could be another causal path, independent of the neural/physical causal chain, that connects the desire to the leg movement. It seems then that if a neural event in the motor cortex is the ultimate physical cause of the leg movement, my desire must somehow cause that neural event. But how is that possible?

Much is known about the physicochemical processes involved in the firing of a bundle of neural fibers—how electrical potential builds up in a neuron until it reaches a critical point and then discharges. The rising of electric potential involves the movement of electrically charged molecules; if some nonphysical causal agent is to cause a neuron to fire, it must be able to causally influence the motion of molecules. I assume we know something about how molecular motions take place inside a cell, what physical forces are active in causing these motions, and just how the motions depend on the magnitudes of these forces. Do we really have any conception of how some immaterial, nonphysical force might change the motion of even a single molecule, causing it to speed up or slow down, or change its direction? Will brain scientists ever look for nonphysical forces, or nonphysical phenomena, to explain some neural event for which they are having difficulty identifying a physical cause? If they should decide to do that, how would they go about it? Where and how would they look for nonphysical causes of neural events? How would they identify one and measure its properties?

The answer of course is that brain scientists will not look outside the physical domain for explanations of neural phenomena. They are not likely to think that it will be scientifically productive to look for nonphysical, immaterial forces to explain neural events. We expect the physical world to be causally self-contained and explanatorily self-sufficient. That is, we suppose that if a neural event—or more broadly, a physical event—has a cause, or an explanation, then it must have a physical cause and a physical explanation. This is the principle of causal/explanatory closure of the physical domain.

Some dualists may think that these considerations are question-begging in that they assume the causal closure of the physical. There are excellent, even compelling, reasons for accepting the causal and explanatory self-sufficiency of the physical world,[2] but rather than arguing this point, let me show you another way of generating the problem of mental causation for property dualists. Consider a mental event, say an occurrence of pain. We believe—in fact, we know—that pain occurs only because a certain neural state, call it ψ, occurs. ψ may differ from organism to organism, especially in organisms belonging to different biological species, but we do not think that there are sensations that float free from the brain, without being grounded in underlying neural processes. Assume that ψ is the neural substrate of pain in you: If ψ occurs, you will experience pain, and you will not experience pain unless ψ occurs. Consider the claim that the pain caused your finger to twitch. Suppose, further, that neurophysiologists have discovered a causal chain from ψ, the neural substrate of your pain, to the finger twitching, establishing ψ as its sufficient physical cause. I believe the existence of such a causal chain is highly likely; we already know a lot about physical causal processes underlying many sensory processes. This means that your finger twitching has two putative causes, one mental (your pain) and one physical (the pain's neural substrate ψ). Given that your finger twitching, a physical event, has a full physical cause, how is a mental cause also possible? How could one and the same event have two distinct causal origins? Doesn't the physical cause threaten to preempt the supposed mental cause? This is the problem of causal exclusion, as may be recalled. Note that in developing this problem, we have used various highly plausible empirical assumptions about the neurophysiology of pain (along with some commonsensical assumptions about causality), but not the principle of physical causal closure.

2. For further discussion, see David Papineau, "The Rise of Physicalism," in *Physicalism and Its Discontents*, ed. Carl Gillett and Barry Loewer (Cambridge: Cambridge University Press, 2001).

It is clear that property dualism has no way of dealing with these questions, and that, especially in view of physical causal closure, phenomena outside the physical domain must remain causally impotent, mere epiphenomena, at least with regard to physical phenomena. In 1970, Donald Davidson's "Mental Events"[3] appeared, and this influential paper sparked the revival of the problem of mental causation, more than three hundred years after the problem doomed Descartes's interactionist dualism. What has become increasingly evident over the past thirty years is that mental causation poses insuperable difficulties for all forms of mind-body dualism—for property dualism no less than substance dualism. Some philosophers are still gamely holding on, trying to somehow fashion an account of mental causation within the nonreductive scheme, but I believe that if we have learned anything from the three decades of debate, it is the simple point that unless we bring the supposed mental causes fully into the physical world, there is no hope of vindicating their status as causes, and that the reality of mental causation requires reduction of mentality to physical processes, or of minds to brains.

PHYSICALISM AT A CROSSROADS

In getting to where we are at this point, the first choice point we faced was where we had to decide between substance dualism, which posits both material bodies and immaterial minds, and ontological physicalism, which admits only material objects. Motivations for introducing entities other than material things vary— from supposed philosophical requirements in connection with certain issues, for example, the persistence of persons over time, a possible survival of bodily death, and the special directness of knowledge of one's own mind, to religious imperatives and mystical intimations. As we saw, however, immaterial minds,

3. In Donald Davidson, *Essays on Actions and Events* (Oxford and New York: Oxford University Press, 1980); first published in 1970.

outside physical space, are causally cut off not only from physical objects and events but also from other minds as well. Each immaterial mind would be a totally isolated entity; its existence is inexplicable and its presence or absence can make no difference to anything else. I believe this is sufficient ground for rejecting substance dualism of all kinds, or any ontology that acquiesces in immaterial, nonphysical things. The alternative is physicalism with an ontology countenancing only material things. There is just one kind of substance, and it is material substance. The physical world of spacetime is the whole world.[4]

Let us suppose then that at the first choice point we have opted for ontological physicalism. The next choice point we face concerns the properties of material things: Given that only material things exist, what kinds of properties do they, or can they, have? Specifically, can they have properties that are not physical? That is, can they have properties that are not dealt with in fundamental physics or reducible, in some broad but clear sense, to fundamental physical properties? As we saw, many thinkers have been attracted to an affirmative answer to this question, holding the view that complex physical systems can exhibit novel, "emergent" properties that are not reducible to the properties of their simpler constituents. Early emergentists thought that even such simple physicochemical properties as the transparency of water were emergent; now it is generally conceded that consciousness and mentality are the best, and perhaps the only, candidates for genuine emergence.[5] Emergentism, which is now showing signs of a revival after having been moribund for much of the second half of the twentieth century, is a form of property dualism, the position that, in

4. What of abstract things, like numbers, properties, propositions, and the like? I am concerned here only with the concrete world; I am setting aside the issue of Platonic objects, although some philosophers believe that Platonism is excluded by naturalism.

5. There have recently been various attempts to devise a notion of emergence which might be usefully applied to purely physical situations (as well as

addition to physical properties, there are physically irreducible domains of emergent properties, of which mental properties are among the leading candidates. Other forms of antireductionism include Davidson's "anomalous monism" and the early functionalism of Hilary Putnam and Jerry Fodor. Property dualism based on ontological physicalism is called nonreductive materialism (or physicalism). Emergentism, anomalous monism, and Putnam-Fodor functionalism are the best-known examples of nonreductive materialism.[6]

What we have just seen is that this intermediate halfway house between the two poles of substance dualism and reductionist physicalism is a promissory note that cannot be redeemed. As we saw, the supervenience/exclusion argument shows that property dualism is not able to explain how mental causation is possible; instead of saving mental causation, it ends up relegating mental phenomena to the status of epiphenomena. Nonreductive materialism has been motivated by a desire to save mentality as something distinctive and special, and something that we value. Instead of saving it, it loses it by depriving it of causal powers. The important lesson we have learned from three decades of debate—Davidson's "Mental Events" was published in 1970—is this: the demands of causality do not tolerate duality of properties any more than duality of substances, and both Cartesian substance dualism and contemporary property dualism run aground on the rocks of mental causation.

---

mentality). See, e.g., Paul Humphreys, "How Properties Emerge," *Philosophy of Science* 64 (1997): 53–70; Alexander Rueger, "Robust Supervenience and Emergence," *Philosophy of Science* 67 (2000): 466–89, and "Physical Emergence, Diachronic and Synchronic," *Synthese* 124 (2000): 297–322; David Newman, "Emergence and Strange Attractors," *Philosophy of Science* 63 (1996): 246–61; Michael Silberstein, "Converging on Emergence," *Journal of Consciousness Studies* 8 (2001): 62–98.

6. The qualifier "Putnam-Fodor" is needed because functionalism of the kind advocated by David Armstrong and David Lewis cannot be viewed as a form of property dualism, at least not in a straightforward way.

So property dualism is out—at least, for now. Where do we go from here? If causality excludes dual realms of mental and physical properties, that means that there is only one secure causal domain, the domain of physical properties. What then happens to mental properties? One possibility is that mental properties are reducible to physical properties: if mental properties are reduced to physical properties, this would conserve and legitimatize them as members of the physical domain, thereby safeguarding their causal status. But suppose that the mental fails to reduce: we would then be faced with the specter of epiphenomenalism, and we must find a way to live with causally impotent mental properties. This may very well push us over the edge into mental irrealism; for one might argue that epiphenomenalism is a fate no better than irrealism and in fact indistinguishable from it—Samuel Alexander urged that to deprive something of causal powers is to deprive it of existence.[7] This leads to eliminativism: mental properties are banished from our ontology as causally idle "danglers" with no purpose to serve. This is not an outcome that anyone can welcome; most philosophers—for example, Jerry Fodor as we will see below—take mental causation as wholly nonnegotiable; it must be protected at all costs. The best, or the most satisfying, outcome would have been a vindication of mental causation along the lines of nonreductive physicalism; that would have allowed us to retain mentality as something that is causally efficacious and yet autonomous vis-à-vis the physical domain.

But the best outcome, as we saw, is not to be had. The next best outcome, in fact our only hope at this point if mental causation is to be saved, is physical reductionism. Physical reduction would save causal efficacy for mentality, at the cost of its autonomy. Reductionism allows only one domain, the physical domain, but the mental may find a home in that domain. Some

---

7. Samuel Alexander, *Space, Time and Deity* (London: Macmillan, 1927), vol. 2, p. 8.

will say that the reductionist option is hardly distinguishable from eliminativism, that to reduce minds and consciousness to patterns of electrical activity in a network of soulless neurons is in effect to renounce them as a distinctive and valued aspect of our being. This reaction is understandable but inappropriate. There is an honest difference between elimination and conservative reduction. Phlogiston was eliminated, not reduced; temperature and heat were reduced, not eliminated. Witches were eliminated, not reduced; the gene has been reduced, not eliminated. We have a tendency to read "nonphysical" when we see the word "mental," and think "nonmental" when we see the word "physical." This has the effect of making the idea of physical reduction of the mental a simple verbal contradiction, abetting the idea that physical reduction of something we cherish as a mental item, like thought or feeling, would turn it into something other than what it is. But this would be the case only if by "physical" we meant "nonmental." We should not prejudge the issue of mind-body reduction by building irreducibility into the meanings of our words. When we consider the question whether the mental can be physically reduced, it is not necessary—even if this could be done—to begin with general definitions of mental and physical; rather, the substantive question that we are asking, or should be asking, is whether or not things like belief, desire, emotion, and consciousness are reducible to neural, biological, and physico-chemical properties and processes. We can understand this question and intelligently debate it, without subsuming these items under some general conception of what it is for something to be mental. If "mental" is understood to imply "nonphysical," it will then be an open question whether or not belief, desire, sensation, perception, and the rest are mental in that sense. And this question will replace the original question of their physical reducibility. There is here a substantive question which no verbal conventions or decisions should be allowed to trivialize.

In any case, our best remaining option is reductionism. Does this mean that we are committed willy-nilly to reductionism? The answer is no: what we have established, if our considerations have been generally correct, is a *conditional* thesis, "If mentality is to have a causal influence in the physical domain—in fact, if it is to have any causal efficacy at all—it must be physically reducible." I have not argued for reductionism simpliciter; rather, I have argued that mental causation requires reduction, and that anyone who believes in mental causation must be prepared to endorse mind-body reduction. We may call this "conditional reductionism." It is important to keep in mind that this is not reductionism *tout court*. Moreover, none of this says anything about the truth or plausibility of reductionism. Whether or not the mental can be reduced to a physical base is an independent question that must be settled on its own merits. Those of us who believe in mental causation should hope for a successful reduction. But again this is only a wish; it doesn't make reducibility real or reductionism true.[8]

So we have finally come to a crossroads: Can we physically reduce minds? Is mentality reducible in physical terms?

REDUCING MINDS

In raising this question about the reducibility of the mental, it is important not to think that the mental as a totality must be either all reducible or all irreducible. It may well be that parts of the mental are reducible while the rest is not. It may be that

8. I have sometimes been described as a reductionist (for example, Robert Van Gulick refers to me as a "hard core reductive materialist" in his survey article "Reduction, Emergence and Other Recent Options on the Mind-Body Problem: A Philosophical Overview," *Journal of Consciousness Studies* 8 (2001): 1–34, p. 2. I am sure I have often written and spoken in confusing ways in the past, but I hope this sets the record straight.

the physicalist project can be carried through for various sub-domains of the mental but not for all, and that physicalism can be vindicated for much of the world but not for the whole world. I will argue that this is in fact the case, namely that much of the mental domain can be physicalized but not all of it. More specifically, my view is that the qualitative characters of conscious experience, what are now commonly called "qualia," are irreducible, but that we have reason to think that the rest, or much of it anyway, is reducible. I am of course not the first, or only, person to hold a view like this; Joe Levine, David Chalmers, and others have argued, quite plausibly in my opinion, for just such a position.[9]

Chalmers distinguishes between two classes of mental states, those he calls "psychological" and those he calls "phenomenal." Psychological states are states that "play the right sort of causal role in the production of behavior,"[10] and include states like belief, desire, memory, and perception. I will call them "intentional/cognitive properties." Phenomenal states are states with a qualitative character—or, to use a phrase popularized by Thomas Nagel, states such that there is "something it is like" to be in those states—like pain, itch, the visual experience of yellow when you look at a field of sunflowers, and the tactile sensation you experience when you run your fingers over a smooth marble surface. On Chalmers's view, intentional/cognitive properties are physically reducible, whereas phenomenal properties, or "qualia," resist reduction.[11]

9. Joseph Levine, "On Leaving Out What It's Like," in *Consciousness*, ed. Martin Davies and Glynn W. Humphreys (Oxford: Blackwell, 1993); David Chalmers, *The Conscious Mind* (New York: Oxford University Press, 1996); see especially ch. 3.

10. Chalmers, *The Conscious Mind*, p. 11.

11. Chalmers would put this in terms of reductive explanation, not reduction. However, his concept of reductive explanation closely corresponds to my notion of reduction; on the functional model of reduction that I favor, reductive explanation is not separable from reduction. See chapter 4 for details.

But what is it to "reduce" something? What needs to be done to accomplish a physical reduction of something mental?[12] Consider the gene and how it has been reduced in molecular biology. The concept of a gene is the concept of a mechanism in an organism that encodes and transmits genetic information. That, I believe, was indeed the concept that Mendel, the founder of modern genetics, had in mind when he spoke of "genetic factors." Genetic factors were to be whatever mechanisms or processes in organisms were causally responsible for the transmission of heritable characteristics. In short, the concept of a gene is defined in terms of a causal function, or causal role—in terms, that is, of the causal task that must be performed by whatever it is that is to qualify as a gene. As we will say, the concept of a gene is a "functional" concept, and the property of being a gene is a functional property defined by a "job description." A functional conception of the gene defines the scientific research program: Identify the mechanisms—say, in pea plants or fruit flies or whatever—that perform the task of transmitting heritable characteristics. Research in molecular genetics has shown, we are told, that it is DNA molecules that perform this task—they are the genes we have been looking for. That is to say, the DNA molecules are the "realizers" of the gene. Moreover, molecular genetics provides us with an explanation of how DNA molecules manage to perform this complex causal work. When all this is in, we can say that the gene has been physically reduced, and that we now have a reductive explanation of how the process of heredity works at the molecular level. Notice that while, as far as we know, DNA molecules are the genes for terrestrial life, there is no reason to presume that they are the only possible physical mechanisms capable of performing the causal tasks associated with the concept of a gene. It might well be that in certain extraterrestrial organisms these tasks are performed

12. Reduction was discussed earlier in greater detail; see chapters 1 and 4.

not by DNA molecules but by molecules of another kind, say XYZ; for them, XYZ molecules, not DNA molecules, would be the genes. This sort of "multiple realization" must be expected, but the phenomenon of multiple realization, whether actual or only nomologically possible, does not, as some philosophers used to assume, represent an impediment to reduction or reductive explanation.[13]

To summarize, then, reduction can be understood as consisting of three steps: The first is a conceptual step of interpreting, or reinterpreting, the property to be reduced as a functional property, that is, in terms of the causal work it is supposed to perform. Once this has been done, scientific work can begin in search of the "realizers" of the functional property—that is, the mechanisms or properties that actually perform the specified casual work—in the population of interest to us. The third step consists in developing an explanation at the lower, reductive level of how these mechanisms perform the assigned causal work. When the first step has been carried out and the property targeted for reduction has been functionalized, in an important sense the property has been shown to be "reducible"—it is now a matter of scientific research to find the realizers. That is, if anything has the functionalized property, it follows that it instantiates some lower-level physical realizer, and it must in principle be possible for scientific investigation to identify it. Even if we have not identified the actual realizer—perhaps we never will—it would make not much difference philosophically: we know that there must be a lower-level physical realizer, even if we don't have a perspicuous description of it in an underlying theory, and we know the phenomenon involved to be reducible to its physical realizer, whatever it is. This means that as far as the metaphysical

13. On this issue, see my "Multiple Realization and the Metaphysics of Reduction," reprinted in *Supervenience and Mind* (Cambridge: Cambridge University Press, 1993), and *Mind in a Physical World* (Cambridge, MA: MIT Press, 1998).

situation is concerned the functional definability of a property is the only issue that matters. That a property is functionalizable—that is, it can be defined in terms of causal role—is necessary and sufficient for functional reducibility. It is only when we want to claim that the property has been *reduced* (for a given system) that we need to have identified its physical realizer (for that system).

Our question about reduction of minds, therefore, comes to this: Are mental properties functionalizable? Can they be defined or characterized in terms of their causal work? The answer, as I have indicated, is yes and no. No for qualitative characters of experience, or "qualia," and yes, or probably yes, for the rest.

Why should we think that intentional/cognitive properties like believing, desiring, and intending are functionally definable, in terms of the work they do? I do not believe that anyone has produced full functional definitions for them, and it is perhaps unlikely that we will have such definitions any time soon. However, there are various considerations that indicate that these properties are functional properties and should be characterizable in terms of the causal work they do in the overall economy of human behavior. Consider a population of creatures, or systems, that are functionally and behaviorally indistinguishable from us, and, in general, observationally indistinguishable from us. Exact indistinguishability or indiscernibility is unimportant; we may simply suppose that their behaviors are largely similar to ours. They interact with their physical environment, which we may suppose is pretty much like ours, and interact with one another, much the same way we do. In particular, they exhibit similar linguistic behavior; as far as we can tell, they use language as we do for expressive and communicative purposes. If all this is the case, it would be incoherent to withhold states like belief, desire, knowledge, action, and intention from these creatures. If, for example, we grant that these creatures are language users, that alone would be sufficient to qualify them as creatures with thought, belief, understanding, intentionality, meaning, and the rest. Assertion is fundamental to speech, and a language user must be capable of making assertions. When someone makes an assertion, he expresses a belief. When someone asks a question or gives a command, he is expressing a thought and a desire. A language user is a cognitive being with full intentionality. And if we grant agency to these creatures (how could we not, given that they have belief and desire, and that their observable behavior is like ours?), we will be compelled to see them as creatures with desires, preferences, and intentions, and whose behavior and actions can be evaluated according to the norms of rationality. It seems to me that we cannot avoid thinking of intentional/ cognitive states, like thought, belief, and desire, as supervenient on behavior and other observable physical facts. We must accept creatures that are behaviorally and functionally like us as creatures with a mentality similar to ours—with belief, desire, intentionality, will, and so on. This is one strong reason for thinking that such mental properties are definable and interpretable in terms of their roles in behavior causation.

Looking at the situation less globally, suppose that we are told to create a device that perceives shapes and colors of medium-sized objects presented to it (perception), processes and stores the information so gained (belief, memory, knowledge), and uses it to guide its actions (agency). I believe we know how to go about designing and building machines with such capacities; in fact, I believe simple machines with such powers have already been manufactured. That is because these states and processes, like perception, belief, memory, and using information to guide action, are specifiable in terms of their causal roles, or "job descriptions." A creature, or system, that has the capacity to do certain things in certain ways under certain conditions is ipso facto something that perceives, remembers, and appropriately behaves. I believe this is why mental talk comes so naturally in describing the activities and capacities of certain artifacts; we talk of a radar system "mistaking" a weather balloon for an approaching airliner, a chess-playing computer as "trying to capture" an enemy pawn, and even the humble supermarket automatic door opener as "seeing" or "knowing" that a customer is approaching. Mental talk is even more natural and familiar for animals—not only dogs and cats, but also those farther removed from us, say, mollusks and insects and even amoebas.

These are among the reasons for thinking that cognitive/intentional mental properties are closely tied, conceptually and semantically, to behavior. This does not mean that we are now, or ever will be, in a position to produce neat functional definitions for complex and multifaceted capacities and properties like belief, desire, and emotion. Logical behaviorists and functionalists are widely thought to have failed to deliver such definitions. But that is not crucial. I think the following two facts are important in this context: First, partial functional analyses of these properties in terms of their causal work, even if complete analyses are not available, can get us going with the scientific projects of searching for the underlying physical/biological mechanisms. We don't have to know all the things that belief does before we start work on uncovering its possible neural mechanisms; a partial list will be enough to start us off. The list will grow richer and more detailed, and this will provide directions for further scientific work. Second, the fact is that even though a complete analysis of belief is not in and perhaps never will be, we don't think there is ultimately anything beyond causal work vis-à-vis observable behavior that is involved in belief. To be sure, beliefs can generate further beliefs; in conjunction with desires, they can cause further desires; and so on. However, these further mental states, too, must ultimately be anchored, conceptually and epistemologically, in observable behavior. In looking for causal mechanisms that ground beliefs, these causal connections with other mental states must be accounted for and identified. This only means that the identification of the realizers of belief must go hand in hand with the identification of realizers of these other mental states. And research results at the level of realizers may lead to the reshaping of the higher-level mental concepts in various ways. As far as intentional states are concerned, we are within the domain of behavior and the physical mechanisms involved in their production; they do not take us outside this domain.[14]

Let us now turn to sensory states. Can we reduce qualitative states of consciousness?[15] Suppose we are given another engineering project. This time, we are asked to design a machine that responds to punctures and abrasions to its own skin ("tissue damage") by taking evasive maneuvers to separate itself from the source of the damage ("escape behavior"); in addition, we are told to make this device experience pain when it suffers damage to its skin. That is, we are asked to design into the machine a "pain box" which, in addition to its causal work of triggering an appropriate motor response when it suffers damage, gives rise to a pain experience. We can, I am sure, easily design into a machine a device that will serve as a causal intermediary between the physical input and the behavior output, but making it experience pain is a totally different affair. I don't think we even know where to begin. What we miss, something that we need to know in order to design a pain-experiencing machine, is a connection between the causal work of the pain box and the arising of pain when the box is activated. Why pain rather than itch or tickle? The machine would try to flee when its skin is punctured even if we had, wittingly or unwittingly, designed itch or tickle into the box.

14. This can be considered a reply to Block and Stalnaker, who argue, in "Conceptual Analysis, Dualism, and the Explanatory Gap," that functional reduction is hopeless because functional definitions of psychological states are not available and never will be. See chapter 4.

15. I have already argued for a negative answer (in chapter 1); here we will briefly go over the same ground but introduce a few new considerations, though no new argument.

What this shows is that we cannot distinguish pain from itch or other sensations by their causal work; our strong intuition is that even if pain is associated with scratching behavior (like itch) or squirming behavior (like tickle), as long as it is felt as pain—as long as it hurts—it is pain. Pain may be associated with certain causal tasks, but these tasks do not define or constitute pain. Pain as a sensory quale is not a functional property. In general, qualia are not functional properties. As far as we now know, the only way to create a system with conscious experience is to duplicate an appropriate animal or human brain.

Some philosophers have invoked the conceivability of "zombies" to show that qualia are not logically supervenient on physical/biological facts. Zombies are creatures that, though physically (hence also functionally and behaviorally) indistinguishable from us, have no conscious experience. The zombie hypothesis has been controversial;[16] less controversial is the qualia inversion hypothesis, namely the possibility of creatures like us, perhaps other human beings, whose quality space is inverted with respect to ours—who, for example, when they look at mounds of lettuce, experience a color quale of the kind we experience when we look at ripe tomatoes, and who, when they look at ripe tomatoes, sense the color that we sense when we look at lettuce. Such spectrum-inverted people would be as

16. In fact, I believe the zombie hypothesis is untenable; Chalmers-style zombies are not conceptually possible. My reason is based on what Chalmers calls "the paradox of phenomenal judgments." Zombies are indistinguishable from us in their speech behavior, and we must regard them as genuine language users. Among the assertions they make are "My elbow hurts," "This mosquito bite is really itchy," and the like; they make phenomenal assertions of the sort we make, and do so under similar conditions. Moreover, their phenomenal assertions are not easily isolated; they are integrated smoothly and seamlessly with other parts of their discourse. To hold onto the zombie hypothesis, we must apply a massive "error theory" to these creatures—namely that all their (positive) phenomenal assertions are false. I believe this is incoherent. We must grant that the creatures have inner consciousness, although the qualitative character of their consciousness remains undetermined.

adept as we are in picking tomatoes out of mounds of lettuce and obeying traffic signals, and in general they would do just as well as we do with any other tasks requiring discrimination of red from green. If this is the case, color qualia do not supervene on behavior; two perceivers who behave identically with respect to input applied to their sensory receptors can have different sensory experiences. If that is true, qualia are not functionally definable; they are not task-oriented properties.

So qualia are not functionalizable, and hence physically irreducible. Qualia, therefore, are the "mental residue" that cannot be accommodated within the physical domain. This means that global physicalism is untenable. It is not the case that all phenomena of the world are physical phenomena; nor is it the case that physical facts imply all the facts. There is a possible world that is like this world in all respects except for the fact that in that world qualia are distributed differently. I don't think we can show it to be otherwise.

LIVING WITH THE MENTAL RESIDUE

So what do we do with this mental residue? If we want to keep mental causation, we should try to minimize its scope and impact as far as possible. Can the antiphysicalist celebrate his victory? Hardly. For one thing, the mental residue encompasses only qualitative states of consciousness, and does not touch the intentional/cognitive domain. And it is in this domain that our cognition and agency are situated. Second, ordinary sensory concepts, like "pain," "itch," and the rest, have motivational/behavioral aspects in addition to qualitative/sensory aspects, and it is clear that the motivational/behavioral component of, say, pain can be given a functional account. Third, we will do well to remember that our conditional reductionism still stands: If anything is to exercise causal powers in the physical domain, it must be an element in the physical domain or be reducible to it. This has two direct implications.

First, the mental residue, insofar as it resists physical reduction, remains epiphenomenal. It has no place in the causal structure of the world and no role in its evolution and development. Second, if we are right about the reducibility of cognitive/intentional mental states, we have vindicated their causal efficacy and thereby largely, if not completely, solved the problem of mental causation. Consider Fodor's lament over the possible loss of mental causal efficacy:

> if it isn't literally true that my wanting is causally responsible for my reaching, and my itching is causally responsible for my scratching, and my believing is causally responsible for saying . . . , if none of that is literally true, then practically everything I believe about anything is false and it's the end of the world.[17]

Three mental causes are on Fodor's wish list: wanting, itching, and believing. We have good news for Fodor—his world is not coming to an end, at least not completely, because two items on his list, wanting and believing, turn out to be in good shape. Two out of three isn't bad! But what can we tell Fodor about itching? Should he care about itching, as much as about wanting and believing? At least we can say this: If we can save intentional/cognitive properties, we can save our status as cognizers and agents. Saving itching isn't required for saving cognition or agency.

Actually, though, I believe we can go some distance toward saving qualia, though not all the way. I have earlier noted how two persons whose color spectra are inverted with respect to each other can exhibit the same discriminative behavior. Brief reflection shows that some important aspects of qualia are

17. Jerry Fodor, "Making Mind Matter More," reprinted in *A Theory of Content and Other Essays* (Cambridge, MA: MIT Press, 1990), p. 156. First published in 1989.

quite directly manifestable in behavior and therefore function-alizable. For analogy, consider traffic lights: everywhere in the world, red means stop, green means go, and yellow means slow down. But that is only a convention, the result of a social arrangement; we could have adopted a system according to which red means go, green means slow down, and yellow means stop, or any of the remaining combinations. That would have made no difference to traffic management. What matters are the differences and similarities among colors, not their intrinsic qualities. In fact, we could have chosen shapes instead of colors, with circle meaning go, square meaning stop, and so on. Discrimination is what matters; qualities discriminated do not. I believe Moritz Schlick made the observation that what can be communicated about experiences is their form, not their content.

Suppose that we have already acknowledged that a given perceiver can experience a range of qualia. When we present to her a ripe tomato, we may not know, and may not care, what the intrinsic quality of her visual experience is—what color quale he is experiencing. Similarly, when we present to her a bunch of spinach leaves, we may not know what quale characterizes her visual experience. However, we can tell whether her color quale of the tomato is the same as, or different from, her color quale of the spinach leaves. When we next present to her a head of lettuce, we can tell whether the quale she is now experiencing is similar to, or different from, each of the two color qualia she has just experienced. That is, the intrinsic qualities associated with qualia are, or may be, undetectable, but differences and similarities between qualia, within a single individual, are behaviorally detectable, and this opens a way for their behavioral functionalization.[18]

18. On these issues, see Sydney Shoemaker, "The Inverted Spectrum," *Journal of Philosophy* 74 (1981): 357–81. What I am saying here, I believe, is in line with Shoemaker's view that although "absent qualia" are not possible, qualia inversion is metaphysically possible.

And intuitively that seems right. The fact that blue looks just *this* way to me, green looks *that* way, and so on, should make no difference to the primary cognitive function of my visual system—its function in the generation of information about the physical environment of the sort that makes a difference to my survival and flourishing. Color-inverted persons, as long as they have the capacity to make the same color discriminations, should do as well as we do in learning about the world and coping with it. Intrinsic qualities of qualia are not functionalizable and therefore are irreducible, and hence causally impotent. They stay outside the physical domain, but they make no causal difference and we won't miss them. In contrast, certain important relational facts about qualia, in particular their similarities and differences, are detectable and functionalizable, and can enjoy causal powers as full members of the physical world. But there is a further question: Why are there such things as qualia? Because we need them as place markers; without them there can be no qualia differences or similarities. Without content, there can be no form, no structure. You may now ask: Why are there just *these* qualia and not other possible ones? That remains a mystery; I do not believe that the present approach is capable of answering that question.

WHERE WE ARE AT LAST WITH THE MIND-BODY PROBLEM

I feel that the position I have been describing here is a plausible terminus for the mind-body debate. There are many issues that need to be sorted out in more detail and with greater care and precision; among them are the functional reducibility of cognitive/intentional states, the functionalizability of qualia differences and similarities, whether qualia epiphenomenalism is consistent with the assumed fact that the subject of experiences is cognitively aware of them and is able to make reports about them, and the question whether it is possible to combine qualia epiphenomenalism with full causal efficacy of qualia similarities and differences. But in spite of the further work required, I feel that the remaining work is for the most part a mopping-up operation, and that the important outlines of the position stand out with clarity and salience.

So here is the position that has emerged. It begins by embracing ontological physicalism. Taking mental causation seriously, it also embraces conditional reductionism, the thesis that only physically reducible mental properties can be causally efficacious. Are mental properties physically reducible? Yes and no: intentional/cognitive properties are reducible, but qualitative properties of consciousness, or "qualia," are not. In saving the causal efficacy of the former, we are saving cognition and agency. Moreover, we are not losing sensory experiences altogether: qualia similarities and differences can be saved. What we cannot save are their intrinsic qualities—the fact that yellow looks like this, that ammonia smells like that, and so on. But, I say, this isn't losing much, and when we think about it, we should have expected it all along.

The position is, as we might say, a slightly defective physicalism—physicalism manqué but not by much. I believe that this is as much physicalism as we can have, and that there is no credible alternative to physicalism as a general worldview. Physicalism is not the whole truth, but it is the truth near enough, and near enough should be good enough.

References

Alexander, Samuel. *Space, Time and Deity*, vol. 2 (London: Macmillan, 1927).

Anscombe, Elizabeth. *Causality and Determination* (Cambridge: Cambridge University Press, 1971). Reprinted in *Causation*, ed. Ernest Sosa and Michael Tooley (Oxford: Oxford University Press, 1993).

Baker, Lynne Rudder. *Persons and Bodies: A Constitution View* (Cambridge: Cambridge University Press, 2000).

Bickle, John. *Psychoneural Reduction: The New Wave* (Cambridge, MA: MIT Press, 1998).

Block, Ned. "Do Causal Powers Drain Away?" *Philosophy and Phenomenological Research* 67 (2003): 133–50.

Block, Ned, Owen Flanagan, and Güven Güzeldere, eds. *The Nature of Consciousness* (Cambridge: MIT Press, 1997).

Block, Ned, and Robert Stalnaker. "Conceptual Analysis, Dualism, and the Explanatory Gap," *Philosophical Review* 108 (1999): 1–46.

Bontly, Thomas D. "The Supervenience Argument Generalizes," *Philosophical Studies* 109 (2002): 75–96.

Broad, C. D. *The Mind and Its Place in Nature* (London: Routledge and Kegan Paul, 1925).

Bromberger, Sylvain. "Why-Questions," in *Mind and Cosmos*, ed. Robert Colodny (Pittsburgh: Pittsburgh University Press, 1966).

Causey, Robert L. "Attribute-Identities in Microreductions," *Journal of Philosophy* 69 (1972): 407–22.

Chalmers, David J. *The Conscious Mind* (Oxford and New York: Oxford University Press, 1996).

Chisholm, Roderick, M. *Theory of Knowledge*, 2nd edition (Prentice-Hall, NJ: Englewood Cliffs, N.J., 1977).

Churchland, Paul. *The Engine of Reason, the Seat of the Soul: A Philosophical Journey into the Brain* (Cambridge, MA: MIT Press, 1996).

Cottingham, John, Robert Stoothoff, and Dugald Murdoch, eds. *The Philosophical Writings of Descartes*, vol. 2 (Cambridge: Cambridge University Press, 1985).

Crick, Francis. *The Astonishing Hypothesis* (New York: Scribner, 1994).

Crisp, Thomas M, and Ted A. Warfield. "Kim's Master Argument," *Noûs* 35 (2001): 304–16.

Davidson, Donald. "Mental Events," reprinted in his *Essays on Actions and Events* (Oxford and New York: Oxford University Press, 1980). First published in 1970.

Dennett, Daniel C. "Quining Qualia," in *Consciousness in Contemporary Science*, ed. A. J. Marcel and E. Bisiach (Oxford: Clarendon, 1988). Reprinted in Ned Block et al. 1997.

Faust, C. H., and T. H. Johnson, eds. *Jonathan Edwards* (New York: American Book Co., 1935).

Feigl, Herbert. "The 'Mental' and the 'Physical,'" in *Minnesota Studies in the Philosophy of Science*, vol. 2 (Minneapolis: University of Minnesota Press, 1958).

Fodor, Jerry A. "Special Sciences—or the Disunity of Science as a Working Hypothesis," *Synthese* 27 (1974): 97–115.

———. "Making Mind Matter More," in *A Theory of Content and Other Essays* (Cambridge, MA: MIT Press, 1990).

Foster, John. "Psychophysical Causal Relations," *American Philosophical Quarterly* 5 (1968): 64–70.

———. *The Immaterial Self* (London: Routledge, 1991).

———. "A Brief Defense of the Cartesian View," in *Soul, Body, and Survival*, ed. Kevin Corcoran (Ithaca, NY: Cornell University Press, 2001).

Garber, Daniel. "Understanding Interaction: What Descartes Should Have Told Elisabeth," in *Descartes Embodied* (Cambridge: Cambridge University Press, 2001).

Gillett, Carl. "Does the Argument from Realization Generalize? Responses to Kim," *Southern Journal of Philosophy* 39 (2001): 79–98.

Grice, H. P. "The Causal Theory of Perception," *Proceedings of the Aristotelian Society*, supplementary vol. 35 (1961): 121–52.

Harman, Gilbert. "The Inference to the Best Explanation," *Philosophical Review* 74 (1966): 88–95.

Hasker, William. *The Emergent Self* (Ithaca, NY: Cornell University Press, 1999).

Heil, John. *From an Ontological Point of View* (Oxford: Oxford University Press, 2003).

Hill, Christopher. *Sensations* (Cambridge: Cambridge University Press, 1991).

Hill, Christopher, and Brian McLaughlin. "There Are Fewer Things in Reality Than Are Dreamt of in Chalmers' Philosophy," *Philosophy and Phenomenological Research* 59 (1999): 445–54.

Horgan, Terence. "Nonreductive Physicalism and the Explanatory Autonomy of Psychology," in *Naturalism: A Critical Appraisal*, ed. Stephen J. Wagner and Richard Warner (Notre Dame, IN: Notre Dame University Press, 1993).

Humphreys, Paul. "How Properties Emerge," *Philosophy of Science* 64 (1997): 53–70.

Huxley, T. H. *Lessons in Elementary Physiology* (London: The Macmillan Co., 1866).

James, William. *The Principles of Psychology* (Cambridge, MA: Harvard University Press, 1981). First published in 1890.

Kenny, Anthony. *Descartes* (New York: Random House, 1968).

———, tr. and ed. *Descartes' Philosophical Letters* (Oxford: Oxford University Press, 1963).

Kim, Jaegwon, "Causation, Nomic Subsumption, and the Concept of Event," *Journal of Philosophy* 70 (1973): 217–36. Reprinted in Kim, *Supervenience and Mind.*

———. "Epiphenomenal and Supervenient Causation," *Midwest Studies in Philosophy* 9 (1984): 257–70. Reprinted in Kim, *Supervenience and Mind.*

———. "Mechanism, Purpose, and Explanatory Exclusion," *Philosophical Perspectives* 3 (1989): 77–108. Reprinted in Kim, *Supervenience and Mind.*

———. " 'Downward Causation' in Emergentism and Nonreductive Materialism," in *Emergence or Reduction?*, ed. Ansgar Beckermann, Hans Flohr, and Jaegwon Kim (Berlin: De Gruyter, 1992).

———. "Multiple Realization and the Metaphysics of Reduction," *Philosophy and Phenomenological Research* 52 (1992): 1–26. Reprinted in Kim, *Supervenience and Mind.*

———. *Supervenience and Mind* (Cambridge: Cambridge University Press, 1993).

———. *Mind in a Physical World* (Cambridge, MA: MIT Press, 1998)

———. "Making Sense of Emergence," *Philosophical Studies* 95 (1999): 3–36.

————. "Hempel, Explanation, Metaphysics," *Philosophical Studies* 94 (1999): 1–20.

————. "The Layered Model: Metaphysical Considerations," *Philosophical Explorations* 5 (2002): 2–20.

————. "Being Realistic about Emergence," in *The Emergence of Emergence*, ed. Paul Davies and Philip Clayton (Oxford: Oxford University Press, forthcoming).

Kripke, Saul. *Naming and Necessity* (Cambridge, MA: Harvard University Press, 1980).

Latham, Noa. "Substance Physicalism," in *Physicalism and Its Discontents*, ed. Carl Gillett and Barry Loewer (Cambridge: Cambridge University Press, 2001).

Leibniz, Gottfried Wilhelm. *New Essays on Human Understanding*, tr. and ed. Peter Remnant and Jonathan Bennett (Cambridge: Cambridge University Press, 1981).

Levine, Joseph. "Materialism and Qualia: The Explanatory Gap," *Pacific Philosophical Quarterly* 64 (1983): 354–61.

————. "On Leaving Out What It's Like," in *Consciousness*, ed. Martin Davies and Glyn W. Humphreys (Oxford: Blackwell, 1993).

————. *Purple Haze* (Oxford: Oxford University Press, 2001).

Loar, Brian. "Phenomenal States," *Philosophical Perspectives* 4 (1990), 81–108.

Loeb, Louis E. *From Descartes to Hume* (Ithaca, NY, and London: Cornell University Press, 1981).

Loewer, Barry. "Comments on Jaegwon Kim's *Mind in a Physical World*," *Philosophy and Phenomenological Research* 65 (2002): 655–62.

Lowe, E. J. "Physical Causal Closure and the Invisibility of Mental Causation," in *Physicalism and Mental Causation*, ed. Sven Walter and Heinz-Dieter Heckmann (Exeter, UK: Imprint Academic, 2003).

Marras, Ausonio. "Critical Notice of *Mind in a Physical World*," *Canadian Journal of Philosophy* 30 (2000): 137–60.

McLaughlin, Brian P. "The Rise and Fall of British Emergentism," in *Emergence or Reduction?* ed. Ansgar Beckermann, Hans Flohr, and Jaegwon Kim (Berlin: De Gruyter, 1992).

————. "Varieties of Supervenience," in *Supervenience: New Essays*, ed. Elias Savellos and Ümit Yalçin (Cambridge: Cambridge University Press, 1995).

———. "In Defense of New Wave Materialism: A Response to Horgan and Tienson," in *Physicalism and Its Discontents*, ed. Carl Gillett and Barry Loewer (Cambridge: Cambridge University Press, 2001).

Melnyk, Andrew. *A Physicalist Manifesto* (Cambridge: Cambridge University Press, 2003).

Mendelson, Elliott. *Introduction to Mathematical Logic* (Princeton, NJ: D. Van Nostrand, 1964).

Merricks, Trenton. *Objects and Persons* (Oxford: Clarendon, 2001).

Morgan, C. Lloyd. *Emergent Evolution* (London: Williams & Norgate, 1923).

Nagel, Ernest. *The Structure of Science* (New York: Harcourt, Brace and World, 1961).

Nagel, Thomas. "What Is It Like To Be a Bat?" *Philosophical Review* 83 (1974): 435–50.

Newman, David. "Emergence and Strange Attractors," *Philosophy of Science* 63 (1996): 246–61.

Noordhof, Paul. "Micro-Based Properties and the Supervenience Argument," *Proceedings of the Aristotelian Society* 99 (1999): 109–14.

O'Connor, Timothy. *Persons and Causes* (Oxford and New York: Oxford University Press, 2001).

———. "Causality, Mind, and Free Will," in *Soul, Body and Survival*, ed. Kevin Corcoran (Ithaca, NY: Cornell University Press, 2001).

O'Neill, Eileen. "Mind-Body Interaction and Metaphysical Consistency: A Defense of Descartes," *Journal of the History of Philosophy* 25 (1987): 227–45.

Oppenheim, Paul, and Hilary Putnam. "Unity of Science as a Working Hypothesis," *Minnesota Studies in the Philosophy of Science*, vol. 2 (Minneapolis: University of Minnesota Press, 1958).

Papineau, David. "The Rise of Physicalism," in *Physicalism and Its Discontents*, ed. Carl Gillett and Barry Loewer (Cambridge: Cambridge University Press, 2001).

———. *Thinking about Consciousness* (Oxford: Clarendon Press, 2002).

Pavlov, Ivan. *Experimental Psychology and Other Essays* (New York: Philosophical Library, 1957).

Pereboom, Derk. "Robust Nonreductive Physicalism," *Journal of Philosophy* 99 (2002): 499–531.

Putnam, Hilary. "Minds and Machines," in *Mind, Language, and Reality* (Cambridge: Cambridge University Press, 1975).

———. "The Nature of Mental States," in *Philosophical Papers*, vol. 2 (Cambridge: Cambridge University Press, 1975). First published in 1967.

Rey, Georges. "A Question about Consciousness," in *Perspectives on Mind*, ed. Herbert Otto and James Tuedio (Norwell, MA: Kluwer, 1988). Reprinted in Ned Block, et al. 1997.

Rozemond, Marleen. *Descartes's Dualism* (Cambridge, MA: Harvard University Press, 1998).

Rueger, Alexander. "Robust Supervenience and Emergence," *Philosophy of Science* 67 (2000): 466–89.

———. "Physical Emergence, Diachronic and Synchronic," *Synthese* 124 (2000): 297–322.

Schaffer, Jonathan. "Is There a Fundamental Level?" *Noûs* 37 (2003): 498–517.

Searle, John R. "Consciousness, the Brain and the Connection Principle: A Reply," *Philosophy and Phenomenological Research* 55 (1995): 217–32.

Shoemaker, Sydney. "The Inverted Spectrum," *Journal of Philosophy* 74 (1981): 357–81.

Silberstein, Michael. "Converging on Emergence," *Journal of Consciousness Studies* 8 (2001): 62–98.

Smart, J. J. C. "Sensations and Brain Processes," *Philosophical Review* 68 (1959): 141–56.

Sosa, Ernest. "Mind-Body Interaction and Supervenient Causation," *Midwest Studies in Philosophy* 9 (1984): 271–81.

van Fraassen, Bas. *Laws and Symmetry* (Oxford: Oxford University Press, 1989).

Van Gulick, Robert. "Reduction, Emergence and Other Recent Options on the Mind-Body Problem: A Philosophical Overview," *Journal of Consciousness Studies* 8 (2001): 1–34.

von Wright, G. H. *Explanation and Understanding* (Ithaca, NY: Cornell University Press, 1971).

Watson, Richard. *The Downfall of Cartesianism 1673–1712* (The Hague, Holland: Martinus Nijhoff, 1966).

———. *Cogito, Ergo Sum: The Life of René Descartes* (Boston: David R. Godine, 2002).

Williamson, Timothy. *Knowledge and Its Limits* (Oxford: Oxford University Press, 2000).

Wilson, Jessica. "Supervenience-Based Formulations of Physicalism," forthcoming in *Noûs*.

Index